Cistercian Fathers Series: Number Fifteen

WILLIAM OF SAINT THIERRY

THE MIRROR OF FAITH

William of Saint Thierry

CISTERCIAN FATHERS SERIES: NUMBER FIFTEEN

The MIRROR of FAITH

Translated by THOMAS X. DAVIS
Monk of New Clairvaux

Introduction by E. ROZANNE ELDER

CISTERCIAN PUBLICATIONS, INC.
Kalamazoo, Michigan   1979

This translation has been based on the edition of J.-M. Déchanet, *Le Miroir de la foi*. Bibliothèque de spiritualité médiévale (Bruges: Charles Beyaert, 1946), and compared with the editions of M.-M. Davy, *Deux traités de la foi: La miroir de la foi, L'énigma de la foi*. Bibliothèque des textes philosophiques (Paris: Vrin, 1959) and of the *Patrologia Latina* 180:365-398.

Original title: *Speculum fidei*

William of St Thierry 1085?-1147/48

Ecclesiastical permission to publish the book has been received from Bernard Flanagan, Bishop of Worchester.

Available in Europe and The Commonwealth
from A. R. Mowbray & Co Ltd. / St Thomas House / Becket Street
Oxford OX1 1SJ

Library of Congress Cataloging in Publication Data
Guillaume de Saint-Thierry, 1085 (ca.)-1148?
   The mirror of faith.

   (Cistercian Fathers series ; no. 15)
   Translation of Speculum fidei.
   Includes index.
   1. Faith—Early works to 1800. I. Title.
BX890.G863   1978   234'.2   78-12897
ISBN 0-87907-315-2

Book design by Gale Akins
Typeset at Humble Hills Graphics, Kalamazoo, Michigan
Printed in the United States of America

The editors of Cistercian Publications
dedicate this volume in gratitude and respect
to the pioneers of William of Saint Thierry studies,

Marie–Madeleine Davy

and

Jean–Marie Déchanet OSB

TABLE OF CONTENTS

IT IS AN HONOR and a delight to be able to offer *The Mirror of Faith* in this English translation. I hope that the genius of William of St Thierry gives to our contemporary spiritual renewal movement in the present crisis of faith and love what it gave to the twelfth century spiritual renewal movement: a very explicit intra-trinitarian relationship for the soul based on knowledge and love. I feel that the prayer-life of a Christian today needs to recover a flowing personal relationship with the mystery of the Trinity, not as a theological speculation of the mind but as a whole person integrated through the *affectus* into the relations themselves of the Three Divine Persons. Such is the message of *The Mirror of Faith,* a work that is spiritually and theologically profound.

The text used for this translation was the Latin text that J. M. Déchanet gives with his French translation, *Le Miroir de la Foi,* Bruges 1946. The Latin texts of Migne and M. M. Davy have been used as references. The chapter divisions and titles are my own, although I was influenced by the divisions of Déchanet.

One difficulty in translating William is what to do with the term *affectus*. Rather than attempting any 'trail blazing' in the area of English translation, I chose the easier path of leaving it in the Latin with qualifying footnotes and an explanatory appendix. This approach offers the reader a real feeling and appreciation for this particularly rich and important dimension of William's theology and spirituality that otherwise might pass unnoticed.

This translation would never have been possible without Dr Rozanne Elder's extensive concern and suggestions. It bears her influence. And I am deeply appreciative of her assistance. From my own community of New Clairvaux, I also acknowledge a great dependence on Br Laurin Hartzog for his patient devotion in preparing and typing the manuscript for publication and on Fr Robert Finnegan for his valuable assistance and theological acumen in helping express the concept of *affectus*.

THOMAS X. DAVIS ocso

New Clairvaux Abbey,
March 1978

Only a few years ago the introduction to this english translation of William of Saint Thierry's *Mirror of Faith* would have required an extensive explanation of who the author was. As recently as twenty years ago, most books which mentioned him at all identified him simply as the biographer of Saint Bernard of Clairvaux. A few remarked in passing on unusual features of his mystical theology or even seized upon hyperbolic statements out of context to accuse this ardent defender of orthodoxy of being a pantheist.[1] Now, thanks to the painstaking, if not always concordant, labors of J.-M. Déchanet and M.-M. Davy, and to those dozens of scholars who have eagerly followed them in studying and writing on this once all but forgotten monk, William is recognized as a spiritual master of the first rank, in some ways the equal—in some the superior—of Saint Bernard.

Well trained in the liberal arts,[2] William entered monastic life among the Benedictines, becoming about 1121 abbot of Saint Thierry, some eight kilometres from Rheims.[3] His schooling, wherever it took place,[4] and his monastic *lectio* gave him a broad knowledge and deep love of Holy Scripture and the Fathers of the Church which, like monks through the centuries, he appropriated and repeated in his own works as easily as we today fall to echoing commercial slogans. His initial encounter in middle age with the charismatic Bernard

and the cistercian reform[5] unleashed a theretofore unrecog-
nized side of his psychological make-up—a driving need to
'strip down' spiritually, to cut away all dependencies, even
helpful ones once they had served their purpose, and to con-
centrate his full energies in pursuing the monastic vocation:
seeking the knowledge of God, which he defined as seeing
God 'face to face'.[6] A chronological study of his works as a
Benedictine and as a Cistercian reveals a progressive simplifi-
cation and detachment unmatched even by the great abbot of
Clairvaux. And no work better expresses this than *The
Mirror of Faith.*

Woven into the fabric of medieval ecclesiastical society, the
Black Monks sought salvation for themselves and for all
Christians by maintaining an ancient and honorable tradition,
giving glory to God and security to men through fidelity to
the Rule of St Benedict and to the customs which had grown
up through generations of its observance. The first Cistercians,
reacting against the embellishments of time and sentiment,
had undertaken a corporal and spiritual asceticism by which
they discarded cherished observances, impressive ceremonies,
and architectural ornamentation which supported contemporary monastic life, not because they thought them mean-
ingless—some indeed had altogether too much meaning—but
because they found the very richness distracted them from
the search for God alone.[7] The White Monks had resolved to
return to the fountainhead, to the Rule and the Scriptures
which it summarizes. Having settled themselves in their
austere monasteries in the strait and narrow way set out by
the Rule, they began in the persons of their most articulate
abbots and able writers to explicate these sources in terms of
their own personal experience. Unfettered by archaism, they
strove for primitive purity and created a new tradition.
Fusing the boundless optimism of the early twelfth-century
with ancient wisdom, they revitalized monasticism, and
attracted young men—and to their dismay, women—in
an unparalleled flood.

This Cistercian spirituality suited William perfectly. By nature, he seems to have been a person who needed to simplify if he was not to deviate, a 'loner' utterly unable to compromise. His attack on Peter Abelard in 1140 provides a good example of this.[9] After reading the *Theologia 'scholarium'* and some other abelardian book[10] in the cloisters of the cistercian abbey of Signy to which he had, despite Bernard's counsel,[11] transferred five years earlier, William dashed off a quick monitory letter to Bernard—and, being a practical man, to the papal legate—enumerating Abelard's theological errors.[12] 'As you know,' Bernard wrote back, suggesting the friends meet to discuss the matter, 'I am not used to trusting my own opinion in weighty matters like this.'[13] In a much longer treatise for his instruction, William examined and refuted at length those thirteen propositions which he considered erroneous, precipitating the Abbot of Clairvaux into the sorry episode of Abelard's second condemnation at Sens.[14]

In this *Disputation* William bemoaned Abelard's greater apparent reverence for Plato than for Scripture and accused the scholar of digging out intellectual traps for the unwary.[15] Other than that he confined himself to theological matters and did not question the bases of Abelard's errant teaching. Yet he was not unaware of the difference between Abelard's approach to the knowledge of God and his own, and immediately after penning the *Disputation,* or perhaps after the Schoolman's condemnation, he set himself the task of scrutinizing that faulty foundation. In *The Enigma of Faith* he presented a theological discussion of the Trinity, the chief subject of Abelard's *Theologia 'scholarium';*[16] in its companion *The Mirror of Faith* he turned his attention to the way by which and the extent to which the human person can know God. Abelard casts a long, unmistakable shadow across each, for William, while not mentioning him by name, grappled constantly with his teachings, his approach to revelation, and his uncanny—and to William incomprehensible—academic ability to divorce himself from faith in order to elucidate faith. In William's figure of the proud man standing outside heaven's gate disputing with the gatekeeper over the criteria for entrance, it is impossible not to see Abelard.[17] Master Peter loved dispute, and the scores of students who pursued him wherever he went, even into the wilderness of his monastic solitude, attest to the excitement his method generated. His own fascination with dialectic—logic—was shared, less single-mindedly, but no less enthusiastically by most of his contemporaries, including William and Bernard. In his autobiography Abelard had demonstrated that he could stand back and analyze his own life and misfortunes with the same attention-getting detachment he used in philosophy and theology. He himself censured pseudo-dialecticians who, despising authoritative texts, arrogantly presumed to posit answers their puny reason was incapable of reaching.[18] But asking the questions excited him more than determining the answers. One of William's objections to his method, in fact, was that he slid back from his own hard questions to facile evasions, not determining 'yes' or 'no' but insidiously whispering 'maybe'.[19]

From his exposure to Abelard, William learned several things besides the danger of heresy at the universities. The *Mirror* reflects, in the cloudy way of mirrors, a preoccupation with Peter Abelard. It treats of the theological virtues, faith, hope, and charity—with repeated reference to the sacraments—likely because Abelard had begun the one work we know William read by stating that in them consist human salvation.[20] For the first time in his life, moreover, William came down hard on the primal necessity of submitting to authority, of accepting the discipline of assenting to scriptural revelation before investigating the nature and activity of God. Having from Abelard discovered that well-intentioned and believing Christians could suffer serious and honest doubts, which William thought it would be as dishonest and dangerous to cover over as it would be to entertain, he realized that throughout his life he had himself relied heavily on human reason and had never thought through its proper function. Reason and love, he had written at Saint Thierry, are the two eyes of spiritual vision, and both are necessary.[21] But he preferred to write about love and had never paused to consider that reason may seem to oppose faith, that it may throw up contradictions which undermine belief. Once he had seen Abelard at work, he realized the potential opposition between these two 'eyes'. Perhaps he admitted to himself a tension which had long existed within himself and which he had never before recognized.

In the *Mirror*, too, William drops certain hints about himself. To the surprise of no one familiar with his work, he identifies himself firmly as a disciple of Saint Augustine.[22] He reveals at the same time an easy familiarity with contemporary scholarly *quaestiones:* How does God know? Was the Incarnation necessary to human salvation? How is Christ present in the Eucharist? How is the soul regenerated in baptism? Are there sources of revelation other than the surviving Scriptures? Unless the elusive second book was more comprehensive than the abelardian compendia we have, he could not have known of all these questions only from reading what he had of Abelard's works. Could he have remembered them from his own scholarly training; have learned of them from novices entering the monastery straight from the schools of Paris, Laon, or Rheims; heard of them during abbatial contacts with the school at Rheims, a centre of learning since the tenth century?[23] Might he have encountered them during early studies at his home in Liège? He does not say. Yet he certainly knew them.

Like any educated European in the aftermath of the first Crusade, he knew of the existence of non-believers, not hesitant or unorthodox Christians, but unbaptized non-christians. He tantalyzes us by his use of medical terminology which had filtered back from the East.[24] May this, along with his near contemporary treatise on *The Nature of The Body and The Soul*,[25] be evidence that William had

been set to work in the infirmary of Signy, and so had felt
called upon to acquire a medical education?

A fascination with medicine, and his basic augustinianism,
are apparent in the *Mirror's* teaching. Underlying it is William's conviction that man, the greatest of God's creatures,
made to the image of the Creator and therefore capable of
knowing him, is mortally sick. Human pride, which is
nothing but self-deceit, has led to human ignorance and thus
to blindness and fragmentation. All humankind—not just
bumptious philosophers—suffers this disease. It is a universal
malady which has blunted man's natural capacity for God.
William diagnosed this besetting infirmity as the inconstancy
of human nature, man's fickleness, his vacillation, his
pathetic inability to return in a straight line to God without
wandering off into blind alleys and silly distractions, and, as
part of it, his laziness—physical, mental, and spiritual. Its two
chief symptoms are the yearning of the flesh for gratification,
and the blasphemy of the spirit. Each requires special medica-
tion: the flesh needs the discipline of corporal asceticism and
physical labor; the spirit needs reading, meditation, prayer,
and single-mindedness.[26] Yet, more importantly, flesh needs
spirit and spirit flesh. Despite his habitual preoccupation
with 'the spiritual life', William suffered no psycho-physical
schizophrenia. He knew, and consistently taught, that flesh
and spirit must be reintegrated in the proper order if a person
is to recover the wholeness requisite to salvation, for salvation is the re-formation of the individual to the image of
the God who is perfect unity.

If, as a result of the healing process William sets out to
describe in the *Mirror,* a person is to achieve the integrity
without which he cannot see God, flesh and spirit must sup-
port one another. To indicate the wholeness at which he
aims, William uses the stoic term *eucrasis.*[27] In *The Nature of
the Body and the Soul* he defined *eucrasis* as a balance of the
four humors which serve the physical body, the microcosm,
in the same way as the four elements serve the physical

universe, the macrocosm; by providing the material and the order for life itself and for wholeness. When in the physical body the four humors are perfectly balanced, he wrote in the confidence of twelfth-century medicine, disease is impossible.[28] So too, he infers in the *Mirror,* when body and soul reach *eucrasis,* when they are integrated in the correct, because natural, order, the spiritual disease from which our race suffers will have been healed and each whole person may then look forward to the vision of God for which mankind was created and given a rational soul.[28b]

In the meantime, man has three ways of learning and thereby being healed: acceptance on good authority (faith), analysis (reason), and participation (love). *The Mirror of Faith* is an examination of how these three should relate to one another. Here—in the darkness on earth—he insists from the first paragraph, faith must unequivocally dominate. There—in the vision of heaven—only love will exist.[29] Yet unless we are one of God's very few truly simple souls, we cannot get from 'here' to 'there' without using, training, and heeding 'that part of man by which he is the incorruptible image of God', our rational soul.[30] We may choose to believe and what to believe. We may choose to love and what to love. We do not choose to reason; reason is an irrepressibly curious human faculty. We can only choose what we shall exercise reason on and when we shall restrain it. That decision requires self-discipline of a higher order than physical asceticism, and great concentration.

The first step of our cure, William reiterates with relentless insistence, is and must be faith, because it alone determines the direction our life and actions, our inquiries and love will take. Infirm finite man can know of God only what God tells him. To orient himself towards God therefore, each person must first of all accept in loving trust what God has revealed about Himself. There is, William admitted, a credulous 'faith of the flesh', an acceptance without questions which suffers no doubts, but which also has no hope of, and no desire for, understanding. That does not satisfy most rational creatures. They must go on to the 'faith of reason' if they are to advance beyond rote acceptance of the words of faith to an understanding of its reality. This is the faith which teaches man what to believe and therefore how to behave, what and how to analyze, and what and how to love. If, when doubts arise, one does not indulge in a debate with them but confides them trustingly to faith, the humility indispensible to health results. For the very reason that it is the basis of all subsequent growth and healing, faith is the first to suffer attack.[31]

Why would William have gone out of his way to specify faith as the first step—a step he had always before assumed— if not in response to Abelard and to those like him who, William felt, were speculating in the abstract about the divine nature?[32] Chary of theological inquiry devoid of scriptural foundation, William spelled out his authorities: Christ, and therefore Scripture, and ancillarily the insights of those who by their adherence to its text and their virtuous lives and martyrdoms had glossed it, the Fathers and the saints. One chooses to accept these authorities because one loves the Saviour and does not pettily insist that what God has revealed of Himself meet the requirements of unenlightened reason.

Having grounded his search in faith, he then turned to the critical issue: reason. We have here a fascinating self-portrait of a man wrestling for honest self-knowledge. At times he appears to argue with himself, agonizing over the role of reason which, he had now realized, can both defend and attack faith, and can never be taken for granted. Without absolute trust founded on authoritative Scripture, without the humility that trust demands, reason in its restless instinctive search for truth will easily and unfailingly fasten on false evidence and wander off in pursuit of some limited goal it can comprehend. Relying on the physical senses, as outside faith it must, reason will naturally strike out against what it

faith, and instructed by reason, then becomes man's domi-
nant spiritual sense. Faith recedes as understanding dawns.
'Illuminating grace' is not a bit of theological jargon for
William. For him grace meant very literally God's giving of
Himself to man, God in us, 'more intimate than our inmost
self'.[34] A person perceives God in Christ because God is in
that person. He perceives the Trinity because he somehow
participates in the love of the triune God. For the Christian,
self-knowledge at its deepest level is god-knowledge.[35]
Enlightening man from within, the Spirit draws him ever
closer to God's own indescribable light and allows him to
understand something of it. The person who has prepared
himself by faith, reason, and love, and has prayed humbly for
it, may experience in a sudden flash of illuminating grace a
transformation in which faith is transformed into understanding (*intellectus*), hope into hunger (*appetitus*) and
human love into divine love. William expressed this succinctly
in his disputation against Abelard, when he mis-quoted
Gregory the Great: love itself is understanding.[36] The human
soul can now sense God, because its senses, its ways of knowing, have been transformed into the being they sense. This
transformation is the turning point of William's 'mystical
theology', for 'vision' comes by participation. Faith domi-
nates that part of the ascent to God which man, in grace to
be sure, chooses and in large measure controls. The higher
ascent, given directly by God to whom he chooses, is domi-
nated by the participation understanding (*intellectus*) allows.

As in English *understanding* refers both to the human
faculty and to the state which results from its exercise, so
for William *intellectus* carried two meanings.[37] It could mean
a faculty of the rational soul which encompasses the two spiritual senses: reason and love.[37b] In most of his works this is
how William used it.[38] In *The Mirror of Faith*, however, his
most frequent, almost his exclusive, meaning is the state of
being which follows upon the awakening of this faculty in
the transformation of the spiritual senses. He distinguishes

between an *intellectus rationis* and an *intellectus amoris*—a worthier and purer sense of the soul, he believed—and then proceeds to speak throughout as if *intellectus* meant only this higher sense.[39]

All the time the individual is choosing to believe and to love God, he thought, God the Holy Spirit is patiently waiting, prodding, teaching, drawing. At each step of the way, as a person freely chooses to believe and to analyze rationally what he believes, to direct reason and channel love, he—in William's metaphor—is turning his face ever more towards the face of God. When he has oriented himself totally towards God and has opened himself completely to be healed, then, William taught, God the Holy Spirit may suddenly snatch him from his plodding pathway and let him 'see'. He does this of His great love, not because He needs man's understanding and hunger and love, but because the man needs it to become the person God created him to be. It is this sudden flash of understanding which William calls *intellectus* here. By his own etymology, *intellectus* is an interior reading, *in affectu cordis*[40], of what one has theretofore accepted on faith. It is perceiving the reality behind words to which until that moment one had clung literally.

By *intellectus* William meant not intellectual apprehension, although reason plays an indispensible role in preparing the soul for it, but a new and altered state of awareness. *Intellectus* is not a permanent state, an enlightenment once forever attained, but the opening of a door to metaphysical and meta-rational reality. It is not the culmination of the spiritual quest, but a discovery. William himself warned Abelard, or rather Abelard's readers, that analogies contain within them the danger of clouding more than illuminating truth, for men can seldom resist the temptation of carrying them at least one step too far. But he also knew that men can only express their perceptions through the medium of word symbols, so perhaps he would forgive us if we paused for a moment to compare his use of *intellectus* to the flash of comprehension which Helen Keller called her soul's awakening. Several striking similarities emerge, and one monumental difference.

Into Helen Keller's childhood of isolation in blindness and deafness, indulgence, and frustration had come a teacher who patiently, day after day, disciplined her and, spelling words into her hand, waited for some awareness in her pupil that the pressure of fingers meant something and could open her up to the world of the senses and of the intellect. The child responded with only baffled, uncomprehending mimicry. Then one day, Helen Keller wrote:

> I became impatient at her repeated attempts and, seizing the new doll I dashed it upon the floor. I was keenly delighted when I felt the fragments of the broken doll at my feet. Neither sorrow nor regret followed my passionate outburst. I had not loved the doll. In the still, dark world in which I lived there was no strong sentiment or tenderness. I felt my teacher sweep the fragments to one side of the hearth, and I had a sense of satisfaction that the cause of my discomfort had been removed. She brought me my hat, and I knew I was going out into the warm sunshine. This thought, if a wordless sensation may be called a thought, made me hop and skip with pleasure.
>
> We walked down the path to the well-house, attracted by the fragrance of the honeysuckle with which it was covered. Some one was drawing water and my teacher placed my hand under the spout. As the cool stream gushed over one hand she spelled into the other the word *water*, first slowly, then rapidly. I stood still, my whole attention fixed upon the motions of her fingers. Suddenly I felt a misty consciousness as of something forgotten— a thrill of returning thought; and somehow the mystery of language was revealed to me. I knew

then that "w-a-t-e-r" meant the wonderful cool something that was flowing over my hand. That living word awakened my soul, gave it light, hope, joy, set it free! There were barriers still, it is true, but barriers that could in time be swept away.

I left the well-house eager to learn. Everything had a name, and each name gave birth to a new thought. As we returned to the house every object which I touched seemed to quiver with life. That was because I saw everything with the strange, new sight which had come to me. On entering the door I remembered the doll I had broken. I felt my way to the hearth and picked up the pieces and tried vainly to put them together. Then my eyes filled with tears for what I had done, and for the first time I felt repentance and sorrow.[41]

The new sight which William meant by *intellectus* is no more physical than the one Helen Keller describes, though both writers, significantly, chose that as the best metaphor. Both had reached a sight more penetrating than physical eyes could ever provide. *To see* in any sense meant to William that one's faculty—vision, reason, or love—had brought to the soul information which conformed the soul to the object 'seen'. The object remained the same; the seer changed. In the vision of understanding the soul is quite literally changed to the God it has 'seen'.[42] Human understanding has become divine, and the person seeing has become, however fleetingly, one spirit with God.

The new vision which came both to Miss Keller and to William irrevocably altered the recipient's relationship to the whole world around him, physical, rational, and spiritual, because it had transformed him. For both, dull glimmerings through repetition had sprung through rapt concentration to the vibrant experience of participation. For both, understanding had made authority not a burden but an aid and had brought with it instantly an insatiable hunger to know more

and to share more in his new unveiled world. With the appetite grew sensitivity, receptiveness, and love. Learning became
easier—a joy. After understanding, the seeker finds that
attachment to physical yearnings and rational definitions
fades and, forgetting what lies behind, he strives for God
alone, much as Helen Keller dismissed without a moment's
regret the primitive symbols she had previously invented to
make her wishes known. But Helen Keller had discovered the
world which language unlocks; William had discovered a
world which transcends language.

Barriers remained: continued discipline, frustration, blindness. In William's case, the need for faith and rational investigation continued, but never again did they take first place.
The world of God's reality was never again to be the same,
because the seeker would never again be the same. He had
been transformed by an understanding of Reality.[43]

Far from lightening discipline, *intellectus* demands a yet
higher asceticism in William's teaching than the physical and
mental disciplines that prepared one to receive it. After experiencing this understanding, a person must let go of his
dependence on all externals: all things, all stays,
all sentiments, all words, and all conceptualizations.
All words, William believed, even the words of Scripture, can be made into false gods if a person does
not realize that God infinitely surpasses any verbal
symbol. Words merely point to reality, just as the material
elements of the sacraments point to the spiritual reality they
convey. But as in heaven there will be no sacraments, so too
there will be no words, no faith, no hope.[44] There there is
only the wordless, imageless, inexpressible Godhead whom
only transformed love—of all man's means of knowing—can
sense, for love alone can participate in the God who is a Love
which beggars the word.

In the wake of Reformation devotion to the Word of God,
and Counter-Reformation emphasis on correct theological
formulation, we may find William's verbal asceticism startling

and oddly zen-like. Yet in this, at least, he and Abelard could have found themselves in complete agreement. Cutting through the universalist controversy, Abelard had declared that words function as signs to reality, neither containing nor representing that reality. Anything therefore which men say of God is enveloped in parables and riddles, a pale transference from finiteness to infinity.[45] For William, likewise, a word signifies a reality and evokes its image in the hearer. But God is imageless. Any word we speak about Him is only a vehicle, conveying us from 'here' to 'there'.[46] Once he had discerned the 'there' William, unlike Abelard, lost interest in the word. And he warned that by attaching ourselves to it and refusing to use and then abandon it, we make it a prison rather than a conveyance. Christ came, he reminded his readers, to take away the vanity of idols by showing us God as God is. Himself the Word of God incarnate, he did not come to substitute new idols for old, but to point beyond himself to the Triune Godhead and, by teaching men that the understanding of God is beyond them, to teach them to think and to understand suo modo—in his own way. And when a person has understood this, he has seen in a mirror darkly the imageless and eternal God 'of whom much is said and nothing is said'.[47]

E. ROZANNE ELDER

1.   For example, P. Rousselot, 'L'identification formelle d'amour et d'intellection chez Guillaume de Saint-Thierry,' *Beiträge zur Geschichte der Philosophie und Theologie des Mittelalters,* 5/6 (Münster, 1908), and in *Pour l'histoire du probleme de l'amour au Moyen-âge* (Paris, 1933). Pierre Pourrat, *La Spiritualité Chrétienne, II* (Paris, 1921), 192ff. See too his article 'A propos de la Lettre aux Frères du Mont-Dieu', *Vie spirituelle* 50 (1937) 321-3.

2.   'Chronique de l'abbaye de Signy,' *Bibliothèque de l'école des chartes* 55 (1894) 646: 'in litterarum sciencia peritissimus habebatur, ita ut septem liberalibus artibus sufficenter imbutus.'

3.   For the chronology of William's life, I follow here the reckoning of Stanislaus Ceglar, S.D.B., 'William of Saint Thierry: The Chronology of his Life with a Study of his Treatise *On the Nature of Love,* His Authorship of the *Brevis Commentatio,* the *In lacu,* and the *Reply to Cardinal Matthew,*' Diss. Washington D.C.: The Catholic University of America, 1971.

4.   Emending a defective text in the unique Life of William (see below, n. 33) A. Adam hypothesized that William had studied at the prestigeous school of Laon under Master Anselm (*Guillaume de Saint-Thierry: Sa Vie et Ses Oeuvres* [Bourg, 1923]). He is followed in this by J.-M. Déchanet, who would have William and Abelard there at the same time, and by numerous others. Mlle. Davy, emending the same text otherwise, maintains (as had most seventeenth and eighteenth century references to William) that he had studied instead at Rheims. When all is said and done, we must admit that we do not yet know where he studied.

5.   If, with Fr Ceglar, we put William's birth ca. 1070 and this meeting ca. 1120, William would have been roughly fifty. Adam posited a birthday of 1090 (*Guillaume,* p. 27); Déchanet favors 1085 (*William of St Thierry: The Man and His Works,* CS 10, p. 1), making William in his early thirties.

6.   See *Ep frat* I.viii.26 PL 184:313A (*The Golden Epistle*, CF 12: 18) and I. v. 15; 311C (14): *Spec fid* 4 (CF 15:10), 1 (5).

7.   For cistercian criticism of benedictine, specifically cluniac observances, see Idung of Prüfening, *Dialogue between a Cistercian and a Cluniac*, translated by Jeremiah F. O'Sullivan in *Cistercians and Cluniacs: The Case for Cîteaux*, CF 33 (1977). Saint Bernard's denunciations of elaborate monastic architecture are well known, and often erroneously held up as a blanket criticism of all architectural embellishment. See *An Apologia to Abbot William [of Saint Thierry]* XII. 28 (CF 1:63-6). Aelred of Rievaulx's similar disparagement in *The Mirror of Charity* is quoted in translation in the note on page 67 of the same volume (CF 1: *Bernard of Clairvaux: Treatises I*).

8.   *Exordium parvum, praefatio*, in *Documenta pro cisterciensis ordinis historiae ac juris studio*, ed. J.-B. Van Damme (Westmalle, 1959) 5.

9.   Again, I follow Fr Ceglar's dating. The more generally cited date is 1138, which argues less urgency in Bernard's reaction and more time for him to compose the spate of denunciatory letters he sent all over Europe.

10.   The identity of the second of the two books William said he had remains unknown, despite numerous hypotheses, which I have listed in my thesis 'The Image of Invisible God: The Evolving Christology of William of Saint Thierry' Diss. The University of Toronto, 1972, p. 118, n. 46.

11.   Upon apparently being asked (in 1124 according to Ceglar) to give his permission for William to transfer to Clairvaux, Bernard replied enigmatically, 'It is more advantageous for you and safer for me if . . . you remain where you are and try to profit those over whom you rule'. *Ep* 86; PL 182:210D.

12.   *Ep* 326 (*inter Bernardi*); PL 182:531-3.

13.   *Ep* 327; PL 182:53B.

14.   PL 180:249-82. An english translation is projected in a volume of abelardian and contra-abelardian documents in the Cistercian Fathers series. Some historians never have forgiven Bernard his high-handed treatment of Abelard at Sens. See, for vitriolic example, S. M. Deutsch, *Die Synode von Sens 1141 und die Verurteilung Abaelards* (Berlin, 1880). His dating of the synod has been revised by subsequent scholarship to 1140.

15.   *Adv Abl;* 270D, 276A.

16.   *Aenigma fidei*, PL 180:397-440. *The Enigma of Faith*, translated by John D. Anderson, CF 9 (1974).

17.   *Spec fid* 6 (below, p. 16).

18.   *Theologia christiana* III. 20 (*CChCM* 12:203). Cf. III. 15 (202), Ep 13; PL 178:353-4.

19.   *Spec fid* 11 (29). Cf. *Adv Abl* VII; 276A.

20. *Theologia 'scholarium'* 11 (CCh 12:404). William manifestly knew this work and this passage, for he quotes and criticizes the definition of faith which immediately follows it (*Adv Abael* 1; 249 = *TSch* 12; CCh 12:404).

21. *De natura et dignitate amoris* 25; PL 184:393C. An english translation is projected for the CF series in 1979. Cf. *Spec fid* 1 (4-5).

22. On the augustinianism of William, see David N. Bell, 'The Image and Likeness: A Study of the Mystical Theology of William of St Thierry and its Relationship to that of St Augustine,' Diss., Oxford, 1974.

23. On the scholars at Rheims, see Valerie I. J. Flint, ' "The School of Reims": A Reconsideration,' *RTAM* 42 (1975) 89-110.

24. In his introduction to the translation of *The Nature of the Body and the Soul* (CF 24:28-36) Bernard McGinn traces the probable sources of William's medical knowledge. The translation includes pp. 103-152.

25. *De natura corporis et animae;* PL 180:695-726. *Three Treatises on Man: A Cistercian Anthropology,* pp. 103-152. Dom André Wilmart OSB ('La série et la date des ouvrages de Guillaume de Saint-Thierry,' *Revue Mabillon* 14 [1924] 157-67) dates the *De natura corporis et animae* no closer than ca. 1138, McGinn (p. 28) 'around 1140'.

26. *Spec fid* IX. 12-15 (33-8), X.22 (52). Cf. *Ep frat;* PL 184: 324B; CF 12:44-5.

27. *Spec fid* 17 (43-4). Cf. 13 (36), 3 (8).

28. *Nat corp* 1; PL 696A-7B; CF 106.

28b. *Nat corp* 15; 725C; CF 151. Bell (p. 400, n. 27) cites as a probable source for this important conviction of William, Gregory the Great, *Moralia in Job* 8. 18. 34; PL 75:821. Cf. *Spec fid* 2 (5).

29. *Spec fid* 1 (3-4). William is paraphrasing Augustine, *Sermon* 178, 4 (PL 38:684) whom, interestingly, Abelard had quoted in the *Theologia 'scholarium'* which so irritated William (*TSch* 19; CCh 12:409).

30. *Nat corp* 10; PL 708A; CF 123.

31. *Spec fid* 16 (39-40), 17 (41), 13 (36-7), 20 (50-51), 6 (16), 13 (35).

32. On Abelard's 'abstractionism' see Thomas M. Tomasic, 'William of Saint-Thierry against Peter Abelard: A Dispute on the Meaning of Being a Person,' *Analecta Cisterciensia* 28 (1973) 3-76. Note, however, that in his *Theologia 'scholarium',* Abelard had written (CCh 12: 406): 'Quid enim sperari vel speratum amari potest, nisi prius credatur?' Cf. *Theologia christiana* 3:31 (207).

33. Despite the claim of the anonymous author of the Vita antiqua (ed. A. Poncelot, *Melanges Godefroid Kurth,* I [Liège, 1908] p. 90) that William had a special reverence for Our Lady, he manifested an uncistercian lack of devotion to her, mentioning her only rarely and

then generally to make a point in incarnational theology.

34.   *Spec fid* 20 (49) = Augustine, *Confessions* III. 6.

35.   *Spec fid* 7, 9 (19, 21, 22). Cf *Cant;* PL 184:494A; CF 6:51.

36.   *Amor ipse intellectus est. Adv Abl* II; 252C. Gregory had written *amor ipse notitia est* in *Homil 27. 4 in Evang.;* PL 76:1207.

37.   William also tended to use *ratio* in this double sense, but introduced a distinction between it and *rationcinatio* (the ability to use reason) when he wanted to clarify (e. g. *Nat corp;* PL 180:718C; CF 24:139). Cf. Abelard's definition of *intellectus: Gloss on the περι ἑρμηνειας*, ed. Berhard Geyer, *Beiträge zur Geschichte der Philosophie und Theologie des Mittelalters* 21 (1919) 313.

37.   *Spec fid* 27 (70-71). This is the augustinian use of *intellectus,* which Gilson defines as: ' . . . a faculty above reason because it is possible to have reason without intelligence [= *intellectus*], but it is impossible to have intelligence without reason, and it is precisely because man has reason that he wants to attain intelligence (*Sermo* 43. 2. 2-3; PL 38:254-6). In a word, intelligence is an inner sight. (*En. in Ps.* 32. 22; PL 36:296).' Etienne Gilson, *The Christian Philosophy of St Augustine* (New York: Random House, 1960) p. 27, n. 1 (d).

38.   For example, *Aenig.* (PL 184:404B; CF 9:48): 'nec ea conemur ratione intellectuque comprehendere'; (422D; 84): 'Deficiunt verba, caligat intellectus'; (433A; 102): 'supra omnem sensum et intellectum est [Deus]', but (409B; 57) 'non de sensu seu intellectu Trinitatis', and *Ep frat* (312D; CF 12:17): dabit enim vobis Dominus intellectus.

39.   The translator has done a remarkable job in rendering William's precise terminology of knowledge consistently and clearly in English, a language notoriously sloppy about the very distinctions William makes. By adhering exceptionlessly to a single english word for each latin term, he has allowed us an insight into William's epistemology—at the cost, I am sure, of a great struggle against the temptation to adopt the most appropriate english term in each context. The task was made still more difficult because other modern terms which might have been pressed into service (feeling, experiencing, sensing) already have equivalents in William and meant still different things. Here *cognosco* = to recognize; *cognitio* = recognition. *Cogito* = to ponder; *cogitatio* = reflections. *Intelligo* = to understand; *intellectus* = understanding. *Notificio* = to be aware of.

40.   Only great restraint and mounting page count has prevented me from making a long digression here on the term *affectus.* Wolfgang Zwingmann has written a thorough dissertation on it without exhausting its riches (*Der Begriff* Affectus *bei Wilhelm von St. Thierry,* Diss. Gregorian University, Rome; published Westmalle, 1967 and in *Cîteaux* 18 [1967] pp. 5-37: 'Ex affectu mentis. Über die Vollkommenheit menschlicher Handelns und menschlicher Hingabe nach Wilhelm von St. Thierry,' and pp. 193-226: 'Affectus illuminatio

amoris. Über das Offenbarwerden der Gnade und die Erfahrung von Gottes'). See Father Thomas Davis' appendix explaining why he, very wisely, left the term in Latin in this translation, pp. 89-91.

41.   Helen Keller, *The Story of My Life* (Garden City, New York: Doubleday, 1954) 36-7.

42.   *Spec fid* 27 (71). See also 'William of St Thierry: Rational and Affective Spirituality,' *The Spirituality of Western Christendom,* CS 30: 95-8. Cf. Bernard, *Sermons on the Song of Songs* 62. 5: 'transformamur cum conformamur' (SBOp 2:158; CF 31:156), and 62.7 (SBOp 2:168; CF 31:158). The source is 2 Cor 3:18.

43.   Cf. *Aenig* (PL 184:424B; CF 9:86): 'Et cum efficimur filii Dei, nostra quidem substantia in melius transmutatur . . . . Et cum justus aliquis incipit fieri amicus Dei, ipse mutatur . . . . '

44.   *Spec fid* 1 (3-4). William is paraphrasing Augustine, *Sermon* 158, 4. 7-8; PL 38:684. Abelard quotes this same passage in *Theologia scholarium* 19; CCh 12:409.

45.   Abelard, *Theologia christiana* 3:128 (CCh 12:243); 3:133-4 (245).

46.   *Spec fid* 32 (84), cf. 2 (6).

47.   *Spec fid* 32 (83-5).

WILLIAM OF SAINT THIERRY

THE MIRROR OF FAITH

CHAPTER ONE

Faith, Hope and Charity
Operating in the Soul

MONG ALL THE SAVING ACTS of God, our Salvation,* which our God, the God who saves us, has proposed to man to be observed for his salvation, these three, as the Apostle says, remain: Faith, Hope and Charity.* And they are to be observed in a special way by all who are to be saved. For in the mind of the faithful soul the Holy Trinity has constituted this trinity* to His image and likeness.† By it we are renewed in the inner person* to the image of him who created us.** This is the fabric of human salvation.* All divinely inspired Scripture† watches for its building up and its development in the hearts of all the faithful.

A man begins at faith.* During the time while we pilgrimage far from the Lord,† the Apostle who says that Christ dwells in our hearts by faith* does not deceive us. Yet hope is also necessary for our journey. This it is that consoles us along the way. Take away from a traveler the hope of arriving, and his courage to go on is broken. When we have arrived at where we are headed, faith will no longer exist. Will anyone ask us: do you

*Ps 68:20

*1 Co 13:13

*Augustine, Comm. on Psalms, XLI, 6 and The Creed, Bk 1, 2.
†Gn 1:26
*Eph 3:16 & Rm 7:22
**Col 3:10
*William of St Thierry, Med. Orat., No. 9 (CF3:145 ff)
†2 Tm 3:16
*Augustine, Gift of Perseverance, Ch. 2. Cf. William, Aenig 37 (CF 9:68)
†2 Co 5:6
*Eph 3:17

3

believe? No, indeed! For we will see God and contemplate him. Nor will hope be necessary when this comes about. For when someone sees, what does he hope for?* Yet faith and hope will not vanish but will pass over into their objects when what was believed will be seen and what was hoped for will be possessed. Charity will not only be present, it will be perfected, since what we love in this present life by believing in and hoping for it we will then love by seeing and possessing it.* In the meanwhile, it is easy to see how really necessary are these three powers[1] for the person who desires to move toward that uncircumscribed light.*

Three other things are also considered necessary: a person must have eyes that serve him well so he may look and see.† Now, the eye of the soul is the mind or reason,** pure and purged from all evil. At the beginning, nothing but faith excels it. For if one does not believe that he will see what cannot as yet be shown to a sick soul (for only a healthy soul can see) he will make no effort to recover. But what if one believes he possesses this faith, as I have said, and is able to see what can be seen, and still despairs of being able himself to be healed? Is he not utterly casting himself out and contemning himself? Does he not especially follow the doctor's orders because as a sick man he feels these prescriptions are necessarily harsh? Consequently, hope must be added to faith.

What if one believes that he has all things and hopes that he can be healed, yet does not love,* that light which is promised him? And

*Rm 8:24

*Cf. Aenig 21
(CF 9:53)

*Cf. William,
Cant., Stanza
Seven, no. 80
(CF 6:66),
Gregory the
Great, Moralia,
VI, 37, 38;
XXIV, 6, 11 and
Hom Ezech
II, 14.

†Augustine, Free
Will, Bk. II,
6, 13.
**Cf. William,
Nat corp et an
7 (CF 24:136-8)
Nat am 25; PL
180:393.
Augustine,
Solil, I, 6, 12
to 13.

*William, Nat am
II:4.

what if he meanwhile believes he ought to be content with the darkness which is now, because of its familiarity, usually agreeable for him? Isn't he still spurning the physician? Therefore, a third thing is necessary: charity— and there is nothing so necessary!*

Without these three, no soul is so healed it can see, which means 'understand', God.* Therefore, when one shall finally have healthy eyes, he has only to gaze; as reason is the soul's gaze.† But it does not follow that everyone who gazes can see. A well-directed and perfect gaze, that is, one which precedes vision, is called a power.* Now, this power is a well-directed and perfect reason.† That gaze cannot as yet, although it would like to, turn healthy eyes to the light unless these three remain: faith whereby the gaze must be turned toward the reality which one believes he shall possess, which once seen, will make him happy; hope whereby, when one has looked hard, he assumes that he will be able to see; charity whereby one desires to see and enjoy forever.*

2. The vision of God follows upon this gaze. The purpose of the gaze is this: not that it cease to exist but that it no longer need anything to orient itself in this direction. This is truly perfect power: reason attaining its purpose, which attends the happy life.

This vision is that very understanding, which is in the soul, since it was the soul's function to understand, which means, to see God. Since the upright man lives by faith,* then, these three [powers] remain to form the life of the faithful.† This is why infidels,

*Cf. Augustine, I, 6, 12-13.

*Ibid. The vision of God in faith is the supreme degree of understanding God in faith.

†Aenig, ¶37 (CF 9:68-9). Augustine, Free Will 2, 6, 13.
*virtus
†Ep frat II, IV, No. 203 (CF 12:80)

*Augustine, I, 6, 12-13.

*Rm 1:17, Gal 3:11.

†1 Co 13:13

who do not possess these three as do the faithful, do not follow a way of life comparable to that of the faithful. They believe other things, hope for other things, love other things than do the faithful, and of necessity therefore they live differently. Even if the use of certain things seems to be common to us and to them, we are still using these things very differently, for we orient their use to another goal. We thank God for them in a different way because we do not believe false and distorted things about him. And by not orienting these same things to the same goal but to the goal of the godly and legitimate command, we have the charity [derived] from a pure heart and a good conscience and a faith unfeigned.* The man who relies on faith, hope, and charity, and holds fast to them has no need of Holy Scripture except perhaps better to instruct others. So it is many persons live even in solitude with these three and without books. Because of this, I think, there has been fulfilled in these [three powers] the saying that: prophecies will disappear and tongues will cease and knowledge will run out.* Yet by these means so extensive an education in faith and hope and charity has arisen in these persons that they grasp what is perfect without books, insofar as there can be anything in this life that one can grasp through faith, hope and charity.

3. Perfection in this life is nothing other than forgetting entirely, by means of faith, hope and charity, those things that are behind and pushing on to those that are ahead.* For the Apostle also says: May as many as are

*1 Tm 1:5 and Augustine, Christian Instruction, I, 39, 43.

*2 Co 13:8

*Ph 3:13. Cf. Ep frat I, XI, 40 (CF 12:24)

perfect know this.* Anyone who truly seeks
the Triune God therefore must strive to have
the trinity of these powers in himself and
must eagerly study to conform himself to
their teaching. Consciousness of them is a
paradise of delights* that enjoys an abundance of graces along with chaste delights of
the holy powers. Here man, native to this
paradise, converses with God. He often sees
Him, he often hears Him speaking, he often
speaks with Him.

*Ph 3:15

*Gn 3:8

CHAPTER TWO

The Interdependence of
Faith, Hope, and Charity

WHEREVER THESE THREE cardinal powers are, they are—like any image of the Triune God—so joined and united to each other and among themselves that each one is in all and all are in each one. Thus—what, how much, and the manner in which anyone believes, that and only that and in that manner does he hope for and love. May he hope for what he believes and loves, and may he love what he believes and hopes for. Faith is the name of a power, both a great and a distinguished power. But faith which does not include hope and charity is not a power. Even devils believe. And men who like devils believe, seem to be worse than the devils in that the men are not afraid whereas the devils quake.* Faith must be sure so that hope may be sure, charity sure. As no one can believe without hope, so one cannot hope unless faith is first present, and so hope cannot take another form than does faith. The good that has been believed forms hope's longing because the goodness that has been believed gives the believer the confidence to hope.

*Jm 2:19

In the likeness of the Most Holy Trinity, therefore, faith begets hope, and charity proceeds from both, that is, from faith and from hope, for one cannot help but love what he believes in and hopes for. And in the same way what he loves he also believes in and hopes for. Just as there [in the Trinity] the three persons are themselves co-eternal and consubstantial, so here, too, faith, hope, and charity do not come before or after one another in time. And, as regards the substance of power, they are in some manner consubstantial, although they may appear to have something like personal differences according to the form of [their] respective *affectus.*[2] The usual power of the rational soul is right reason; there are as many species of it as we say there are powers of rational man.

4. There is one form of the power for the three powers of faith, hope, and charity, for everything in this life is based on faith; by it we believe, we hope and we love what we do not see. This is faith and we call it faith. By it we now walk as long as we pilgrimage to the Lord.* In the future life, everything will be called charity both by the grace of the title and because its perfection deserves it since, although faith and hope will not pass away but will pass over into their objects, what we now believe in and hope for we will see and possess. To the extent that one is on pilgrimage through this life to the presence of the supreme truth through an *affectus*[3] for perceiving the Lord in goodness,* faith and hope are sometimes not so much conformed to charity as they are united to it. So it is that

*2 Co 5:6

*Ws 1:1

*Ps 89:15

all three progress in unison in the light of the
face of God,* although the species of its own
unique properties remains to each one. Yet
there often is or appears to be among these
three only the single face of charity. To those
who are clamboring up from this vale of

*Ps 84:6,7

tears* to the height of the promises from on

*William, Cant,
Pref. 6 (CF 6:8),
and Ep Frat,
II, X, No. 235
and II, XV, 257
(CF 12:88 & 94).
Also, Augustine,
City of God,
XIV, 7, 2.

high, this charity, or esteem or love,* begins
here at the stage of faith, when that sun of
justice rises continually† for the person who is
progressing for the first time out of the darkness of unbelief. For he begins not only to

†Ml 4:2

believe in and hope for what he does not see,
but also to love it to the extent that he
believes and hopes. Although the fullness or
the perfection of this love will come to no one
in this life, yet some progress in it must be
hoped for until one finally arrives there where,

*1 Co 13:12

for the person who sees face to face,* there
will be the utter happiness of possessing what
he loved and his every power will be to love
what he possesses.

But meanwhile, faith is for those who
walk: to rely upon it, to breathe it when they
hope to recover from the exhaustion of the
journey and the weariness of the pilgrimage.

*William, Cant,
Pref, 1 (CF 6:3)

The vision of the highest good* forever urges
and draws every rational understanding toward
the understanding and the love of itself. The
closer one gets to it, the purer one will be and
ever the more eager to see what is promised
the blessed pure of heart will see. By faith are
our hearts purified to see what only the pure

*Mt 5:8

of heart see.* This inspires anyone who strives
after loving the Lord his God with all his

*Mt 22:37

heart, with all his soul and with all his mind.*

He influences his neighbor in this as much as he can, for he loves his neighbor as himself. But sometimes, because of the sin of the first man and the punishments of his sins on the sons of his flesh who are likewise sons of grace, there happens what the Apostle records about himself: I am delighted with the law of God according to the inner man, but I see another law in my members warring against the law of my mind and making me a prisoner to the law of sin that is in my members.* *Rm 7:22,23 And also: The flesh lusts against the spirit and the spirit against the flesh.* As long as man is *Gal 5:17 this way, it is clear to everyone that he does not love the Lord his God as he is obliged—namely, from all that man is and from his life [itself]. Frequently he desires very much and very carnally things besides God. As long as he lives here, carnal yearning can be restrained and broken, but it cannot be so extinguished that it does not exist at all.

5. For this reason we are commanded in this life to have that perfect love which is unstinting* and, according to the precept of *Mt 22:37 the law, which we owe to the Lord God. Yet, no one entirely succeeds in reaching [this love]. It is commanded, all the same, lest we ignore the end toward which we must exert ourselves. The more perfect charity becomes in us, the more necessary it becomes that the flesh be lessened until it [charity] be perfected there, where there is no yearning for anything but God. To become more and more perfect in this here below is to walk by faith. When anyone who is making progress in this is found departing out of this life,

CHAPTER THREE

Faith as a Gift

WE DO NOT HAVE a right faith about faith, however, if we do not faithfully understand, above all, whose gift it is. Faith is an element of free will, but of a will freed by grace. The will of a man held captive under sin* can never be free unless he is freed by him of whom it is said: If the Son shall free you, then you will be truly free.* By himself, man is free only to sin. By this liberty all men sin; everyone sins for the delight and love of sinning.* By this liberty the sons of justice have been made the slaves of sin.* They are incapable of freely choosing or of perfecting any fruit of justice unless, freed from sin by liberating grace, they are made servants of justice.* In this matter, deserved justice hardens whomever it wishes from among the children of Adam, who come from the throng of that ancient damnation, by justly deserting that person. Mercy, which is not due, pities whomever it wishes by giving him help.* Whereas anyone who is helped offers a good and free will and accepts faith, anyone who is deserted and forsaken poses questions and deserves damnation. For [Scripture] says: Why is he still asking

*Rm 7:14

*Jn 8:36

*William, Exp Rom, Bk IV, Ver. 13-18.
*Jn 8:34

*Rm 5:18, 21 & 6:20

*Rm 9:18

*Rm 9:19

questions? For who resists His will?* A person who hopes, trembles, whereas he who thus dares, despairs. The one is not asking the reason but imploring mercy. Let the other, who is forsaken, learn from this what he shall deserve unless grace comes to him. As the Apostle says: not all men have faith.* Therefore, who does then?

*2 Th 3:2

The foundation of God stands, he says, having this sign: The Lord knows his own and may all who call upon the name of the Lord depart from iniquity.* For those who are known from eternity in the foreknowledge of God* are the ones who have believed, who do believe and who will believe. These, and none other than these, are the sheep of the Lord, the sheep of his pasture,* the ones who hear his voice, whom no one snatches from his hand,* his people who know that the Lord himself is God.* These are the ones who truly believe, the true worshipers in spirit and in truth,* foreknown from all eternity before they even existed, predestined to be something special, called while they were turned away, justified while they were sinners, persons to be glorified while they were being made immortal.*

*2 Tm 2:19

*1 P 1:2,20

*Ps 100:3

*Jn 10:27,28
*Ps 100:3

*Jn 4:23

*Rm 8:30

6. Known, therefore, and foreknown in the foreknowledge of God, they are aware of themselves even in their own conscience to the extent that they call upon the name of the Lord.* The Holy Spirit bears witness to their conscience that they are the sons of God.* They are made known to men to the extent that they depart from iniquity† before the rest of men. But in a large household there

*Ps 116:17 and
 2 Tm 2:19
*Rm 8:16

†2 Tm 2:19

are not only silver and golden vessels but also
wooden and clay ones. The ones are for
honorable use, the others for ignominious
use.* Why this is and how it is, the potter   **2 Tm 2:20*
decides. He has the right to make from the
same clay whatever he wants to, either for an
honorable use or for an ignominious use. The
thing the potter made does not have the right
to complain to the potter about this, nor
does man to God,* nor the clay to the molder,   **Rm 9:20*
nor the creature to his creator. Since he who
makes all things for a cause or a reason which
he alone knows is Lord of all, he acts freely in
regard to all according to what is good in his
sight. And certainly our good [God] does all
things well.

CHAPTER FOUR

*Faith Implies Humility
and Submission*

J UST AS HUMILITY in the believer is
the most certain sign of a sheep of the
Lord who shall be placed at his right hand,
so also the proud questioning of the
unbelieving person is a sign of the goat who
will be placed at his left.* For with God no
one is saved unless he is humble in spirit; no
one enters through the doorway of faith
except with a humbled head.* The keyhole
of the narrow gate is faith. A camel, a person
who is enormous and complicated, cannot go
through it unless he is shrunken and
straightened to [match] the humility and
simplicity of Christ.* The proud and puffed-
up person comes to the door of faith and
while he is being called to believe and to enter
he stands around and disputes with the doorkeeper about why one person has been
admitted and another excluded until, by the
honest judgment of the doorkeeper, the door
is slammed in his face. And so, debating over
those admitted and those excluded, he finds
himself among those excluded. For he says
about every last thing he does not grasp: This
is a hard saying!* He is harder! And he goes

*Mt 25:33

*Ac 14:26
(Vulgate)

*Lk 18:25;
Mk 10:25;
Mt 19:24.

*Jn 6:60

away and turns back.* He is oriented to the   *Jn 6:67*
things behind him. But the person poor in
spirit—of such is the kingdom of God*—work-   *Mt 5:3*
ing out his salvation with fear and trembling,*   *Ph 2:12*
not opening his mouth against heaven,† comes
and pleads. He prays to be admitted and,   †Ps 73:9
when he is admitted, he worships, always
trembling* and forever in awe of the will of   *Pr 28:14*
the potter who makes whatever he has wanted
from his clay. Even having entered, he is not
secure as long as the senses of his flesh weigh
him down. He catches fire with fear, goes forward with love, burns to understand those
things which he sees, but he is afraid to
scrutinize that which he should not scrutinize.
Therefore, O man, [the fact] that you choose
rightly and that you believe does not depend
on the person willing and running,* but on   *Rm 9:16*
God having mercy!

If you do not choose to believe, you do not
believe. Yet you believe if you choose to; but
you do not choose to unless you are first
helped by grace. For no one comes to the Son
unless the Father draws him.* How? By   *Jn 6:44*
creating in him and inspiring in him a free
will whereby he may freely choose that which
he chooses; this is so that what he chooses
rightly may be of his own will. By God's
inspiration we make a voluntary assent of the
mind to those things which concern Him, and
what we believe in our heart leads to righteousness, but what we confess by our mouths
leads to salvation.* And that is faith. Conse-   *Rm 10:10*
quently it has been said: If you choose, you
believe; but you do not choose to [believe]
unless you are drawn by the Father; and if

you choose to, you choose because you are
drawn by the Father. So examine yourself,
the Apostle says. If you are abiding in faith,
prove yourselves to him. Do you not recognize [the fact] that Christ is in you, unless
somehow you are rejected?* How is Christ
Jesus in us? Through a good will, of course,
for peace comes to men of good will*—which
means by willing that Christ dwell in our
hearts through faith.* For this will is already
to some extent the love of Christ, without
which faith in Christ is utterly impossible.
For devout faith cannot exist without hope
and charity.

Every lack of a good will, therefore, is the
sign of every possible reprobation and obdu-
rate infidelity, just as a good conscience is a
faithful witness from the Lord that we are
sons of God* and of the grace of adoption.
Why do you not believe, O infidel? Surely
because you do not love! You do not believe
because you do not love; you do not love
because you do not believe. The one cannot
exist without the other, for the one depends
on the other. Begin to love; that is: do it so
you may choose to and you will begin to
believe. You will believe as much as you shall
want to, that is, as much as you shall love.
For the will is the beginning of love. Love
then is a vehement will.* And love in the
person who believes will furnish the faculty
for believing.

CHAPTER FIVE

Faith, Which Is Submission
to God's Authority, Needs Love

7. **T**AKE AN EXAMPLE from carnal affection with regard to God the Father. Man believes on the authority of his elders something he learns from no experience: he believes without any doubt that he is the son of his father and mother. The authority of his father and mother, whom he believes, is so innate in him that he has no desire to refute it, because he loves them. Nor can he, for in the judgment of someone who loves them, they deserve it and they seem worthy of being believed without hesitation.* **William,* Nat am, Ch. 7, No. 16. Embrace, then, the grace of divine adoption. You are the heir of God and the co-heir with Christ!* Bend your knee to the Father of Our **Rm 8:17* Lord Jesus Christ from whom is named all fatherhood in heaven and on earth, so that he may, according to the riches of his glory, give you the power of being strengthened through his spirit in the interior man, of having Christ dwell through faith in your heart.* Acknowl- **Eph 3:14-17* edge the dignity of your race, lest you prove yourself unworthy through unbelief. For to deny one's parents according to physical birth is a serious affront to nature. Acknowledge

your mother: grace. Bear patiently that she
may nourish you in the womb of authority,
with the milk of simple history. And suckle at
her breasts so that you may grow quickly.
Grow! Go forward! To shrivel is to fail!

Being born and growing up in a physical
sense is not a matter of will, but spiritual birth
and spiritual increase is a matter of will. In
this the will is the child of grace.* Grace
begets this child, grace nurses, grace nourishes
and carries this child along and leads the child
all the way to perfection. That is: until this
child becomes, like charity, a great and well-
disposed will.* By the workings of a charity
much kinder and more certain than any physical affection, indeed, the Holy Spirit is made
present to bear witness to the sons of grace
that they are the sons of God,* just as nature
reveals to the sons of men that they are the
sons of their parents.

Anyone who believes ought to know what
he believes, who is the author of it and who is
teaching it, that he may believe what he
believes. Anyone who is really a faithful
believer and of good will concerning the faith
never picks out from among the matters of
faith what he wants to believe, but without
any retraction or hesitation he believes whatever divine authority has indicated must be
believed. Nor does he, by devising for himself
new beliefs, savor those things which are, as it
were, more agreeable to his physical sensi-
tivities. Rather he always tries to savor those
things which are true. He applies his reason
to them and studies the doctrine about them.
Nor does he hesitate over them by judging

*William, Ep frat,
Bk I, XXV,
No. 94-95
(CF 12:43-4)
and Augustine,
Against Julian,
III: 19.

*Augustine,
The Grace of
Christ, I:21,22.

*Rm 8:16

them with human reason, but holds them as certain by clinging to them in faith and love. And so it sometimes happens in this that there are those who have faith—a greater than which no one could have—and they are ready to give their life in declaring it. As the Lord testifies: No one has greater charity than the person who lays down his life for his friends.* Yet these same persons in believing, that is, in thinking about matters of faith, are in darkness and struggle. This is the burden and burdensome weakness and astonishing blindness of the human mind. In fact, it is often extremely easy and convenient for many, if necessity or opportunity presents itself, to die for the faith. But it is not easy for them to acquire the purity of the faith itself by believing, that is, by pondering matters of faith.

*Jn 15:13

CHAPTER SIX

Faith and Understanding

9. **N**O WONDER, since those who die most eagerly for the faith are often the ones who find it exceedingly difficult to live according to the faith. So it happens that when matters of faith in Scripture are heard in their historical dimension or interpreted in a moral context by the holy doctors or are touched upon in certain mysteries or sacraments, some persons' perception is at variance and still some others' is wrong. So those matters of faith being preached are accepted by many of the faithful with difficulties and many scruples. Men are animals of weak wit but weaker faith. They do not perceive or scarcely perceive the things of God,* even granted that the reason of faith is repugnant to human reason and human habits. Yet often they are not even willing [to believe], as if they were measuring the infinity of divine power by the infirmity of the human senses or of their own faith, as if (as human nature and its influence suggest) God were able to be or to do nothing except what man all on his own appears to be able to understand about Him, as if the sacraments of faith and the mysteries of Holy Scriptures

*1 Co 2:14

were human inventions.

But the man of faith and power,[4] he who has been predestined to life, anticipated by grace and, like Paul, attended by mercy,* that he may be faithful, although occasionally he puts up with his physical senses in matters of faith, absolutely never gives in [to them]. But as a faithful bondsman of divine authority, he first subjects himself with complete application of his mind to the discipline of the faith which he has learned. Then he strives with all the *affectus* of piety[5] toward that which is given, first to that which flesh and blood reveal, then to that which no one but the Father in heaven reveals;* first to the knowledge which night proclaims to night, then to the word which the day utters to day.* And he is assiduous to learn not only what to believe but also those things which fortify that same faith against the enemies of the faith. In this way faith may come to be where it does not exist and may be strengthened where it does exist. He so guides his life and even his habits that he may not only believe what is to be believed but may hope for and love it, that by loving he may understand and by understanding he may love.* For in this way the spirit faithful to God† deserves the Holy Spirit. Grace merits grace, faith merits understanding.** And the *affectus* of piety and the understanding of love lead every intellect back from captivity into the service of Christ,* so that—as it is written, Unless you believe you will not understand*—the person who believes by loving may deserve to understand what he believes.

*1 Tm 1:13

*Mt 16:17.
cf. ¶16.

*Ps 19:3

*William,
Ep frat,
Bk 2, XIV,
No. 249
(CF 12:92).
†Ps 78:8
**Augustine,
Sermon 126,
1, 1.

*2 Co 10:5
*Is 7:9, LXX.

Gal 3:23 ff.

†*Gal 4:5*

** *Rm 8:15 and Gal 4:6.*

**2 Co 4:4-6*

Formerly, before faith came, we were guarded under the law, enclosed in that faith which was to be revealed, and the law was our tutor in Christ Jesus so that by faith we were justified. But now that faith has come we are not under a tutor* but, having received the adoption of sons,† we have been found sons of God, having received in our hearts the Spirit of God by whom we cry: Abba, Father.** So too in this time of grace, before the light of Christ's glorious gospels may begin to shine in our hearts,* we have to be guarded and enclosed under the authority of that same gospel so that grace may be revealed in us at the time when God's mercy shall enlighten us. In the meantime, therefore, may authority be our tutor in Christ Jesus, so that through the humility of believing we may deserve to be enlightened by grace.

CHAPTER SEVEN

*The Holy Spirit Brings Us Illuminating
Grace Which Is Necessary for Understanding*

ONCE illuminating grace has come we
are no longer under a tutor, for wherever the Spirit of the Lord is there is
liberty.* Having received the Spirit of the
sons of God,* we ourselves are made the sons
of God, both understanding and experiencing
that we have God as a Father. When we have
renounced all confidence in authority, we
may say to that Samaritan woman what her
companions said to her: We no longer believe
because of your word, for we ourselves have
heard and we know that this is truly he, the
Saviour of the world.* Meanwhile, however,
while one is being prepared by believing, that
is, by thinking about matters of faith, it is
necessary that understanding be given its place
so that a great place in that thinking may be
given to authority. In all this, therefore, whatever can neither be conceived by the senses
nor investigated meanwhile by any reason
must be conceded most obediently and believed by divine authority—such as the gospel
narrative of the human dispensation of the
Saviour and his acts, which were done then
for those who were present to see and to

*2 Co 4:6
*2 Co 3:17

*Jn 4:42

believe what they did not see. Yet to us they are proclaimed as something to be believed, because they [the Saviour's acts] were done that way, and through them we are to believe what his contemporaries believed.

But when the temptations of the physical senses—stumbling blocks to faith, sad hesitations, and darkening questions—begin to boil up in the heart, coming not so much from a resolution of the will as from the indifference of a sloppy mind or the shallowness of the normal fervor in our reasoning ability, the faithful soul is accustomed sometimes to being in darkness. The mind believes and commits itself to be ruled by nothing better than the divine authority, [an authority] which divinity constitutes in so eminent a degree of dignity, [an authority] which very many and very great men of God recommend to us by their word and writings, by their life and death. When one has submitted to it with piety and humility, he rests well therein, as if in a safe place, until through the operation of the Holy Spirit, as the prophet says, experience begins to give understanding of what is heard.* [He rests there] until faith obtains that reality which it precedes and enlightens the affection of the one who believes so that from a belief in Jesus Christ there may come to be in his heart both the example of humility and the incentive of love and the sacrament of redemption so that, as the Apostle says, Jesus Christ becomes for him justice and wisdom and sanctification and redemption from God the Father.* Then faith will be really believed. Then one's

Is 28:19

1 Co 1:30

thinking about faith is worthy of faith, although one does not so much think now as act. Whatever faith there is, the Holy Spirit actually brings about in that soul, once the *affectus* of faith[6] glows in the conscience; then illuminating grace flashes in the understanding and the effect of good works shine forth in one's life.

CHAPTER EIGHT

The Temptation of Doubt
and Understanding

11. **I**F WE FORSAKE this guiding authority at the beginning of our believing, we shall necessarily wander off the just way and walk in the influence of our physical senses.* Even some among the ranks of the faithful stumble quite often. Although they do not stumble enough to fall, they are found to pass on not without some danger to life and detriment to a saintly advancement in faith. The fool says in his heart: there is no God;* and someone else says: how does God know or is there knowledge in the Most High?* He has doubts about the providence of God. Someone else wonders if for the salvation of man God ought to have been made man. And there are many things along this line. Even minds quite fervent in religion, but still rather immature in the faith, often undergo this kind of temptation about faith, [temptations] that come not by assailing them openly but by attacking them as if from the side and by plucking at the garment of faith from behind. They do not say: *yes, yes, no, no,** but whisper: *maybe, maybe!* Maybe it is so, they say; maybe it is not!

*2 Co 10:2,3

*Ps 14:1, 53:1

*Ps 73:11

*Jm 5:12

28

Maybe it is otherwise; maybe it is otherwise than written—on account of something that was not written down. When the judgment of reason looks on, all doubts disperse and, although the garment of faith is found intact, it still feels plucked and battered.

In fact, there seems to be a reason which attacks and a reason which defends. The first one thinks things in an animal and physical way,* the other is spiritual and discerns all things spiritually.* The one is, as it were, hesitant about unknown things, the other submits everything to authority. Moreover, it can hardly bear that any doubt should arise in any part of itself. It does not give a doubtful assent to anything [coming] from divine authority and from faith unfeigned.* But what does a spirit do, once it believes in God?* It reads the gospels for itself, the words as well as the miracles of the Lord, and in all of them it venerates and adores the sacred vestiges of truth. When its faith is challenged, it says: You are the Christ, the Son of God.* When its love is challenged, it says: You know that I love you,* and: I lay down my life for you.* And once someone believes all matters of faith with an intrepid heart unto righteousness, let him confess with his mouth unto salvation* on the basis of the law of authority. Nevertheless, if he cannot cut off from the ear of his heart the 'maybe so, maybe not' of murmuring temptation, he does not say this of himself but endures it with great vexation as if it were being said to him by some sort of sense of his soul.[7] He sighs, therefore, at the words of the Apostle, and he is exceedingly

*2 Co 1:12

*1 Co 2:15

*1 Tm 1:5

*Ps 78:7-8

*Mt 16:16

*Jn 21:15
*Jn 13:37

*Rm 10:10

mistrustful of himself: Examine yourselves, he says, see if you are of the faith, prove yourselves! Do you not know that Jesus Christ is in you unless you are somehow rejected?* And elsewhere: No one speaking in the Holy Spirit says anathema to Jesus.* He himself very faithfully added to this: If any man does not love the Lord Jesus Christ, let him be anathema. Maranatha!*

*2 Co 13:5

*1 Co 12:3

*1 Co 16:22

And yet in all this it is not possible to drive out the sting of death from I know not what hidden corner of conscience.* This sting does not pierce but only pricks. Sometimes it does not even prick yet it is not removed. He is very much afraid that Christ Jesus is not in some part of his conscience, especially if there is some part of it which may be opposed to Him, although this very anxiety of fear and sorrow is a manifest argument for faith. No one feels it unless he is fighting and [unless he] already loves what he believes and is afraid of losing what he holds firm, [unless] he is being examined spiritually.* For him the usual habit of assenting and the profession of what one believes is not enough, as it is for many others. He already has enough experience to begin to know what is lacking in himself.* But what is he afraid of in all this? What is he worrying about? What does he grieve over, if not faith?

*1 Co 15:15

*1 Co 2:14

*Ps 39:5

The man of God takes a good look at himself, therefore, and examining himself spiritually he says: What is it, O my soul, whereby you disturb me?* Are you not firm in the faith? Do you not believe? And by proposing these two things to himself, he confers and

*Ps 42:6

treats with himself; he talks over with himself
whatever his heart may reply to him on both
these questions. He discusses what it is and
finds that faith is a voluntary assent of the
mind to matters of faith, but to believe is to
deliberate on, while assenting to them. And
he inspects closely all the limits of his faith
with sincere will in his heart and assent in the
profession on his lips. He finds the works of
faith in his intention and his profession, even
to the inevitability of martyrdom and death
should they perhaps befall him. Meanwhile,
he gives himself a good answer about his faith.
When he reflects on the state of his mind,
just what it is, and when he reflects about
faith, he finds in it indeed a definite assent of
the free choice to faith, yet there is also something in his reflections contrary to this assent.
Discussing thoroughly within himself just what
this is, what he wants for himself, he finds
that the reason simply passes from the obedience of faith to assent, and once the path of
the natural reasoning ability with its doubts
has been abandoned, he finds himself march-
ing along the path of grace, subjecting all
things to authority.

12. And although the mind, detoured from
its natural path and led into the path of grace,
is amazed that it has been led back to its own
territory along another path,* it nevertheless   *Mt 2:12
adjusts itself to believing, that is, to pondering
matters of faith with simple assent. In this
very process, [the mind] suffers the violence
of its own nature reasserting itself and wanting to know where it should assent, even
against its will; it begins to use its reason

CHAPTER NINE

The Trial of Faith

THEREFORE, when faith is proclaimed to [the mind] through authority and it sees itself separated from the end for which it was hoping and blocked off from the path by which it was used to going, it still rejoices that through this broadening there is promised to it the supreme charity of knowledge.* Believing that it will most certainly find there that which is perfect, it has forsaken that which is in part.* Yet when it is meanwhile ordered to place authority before reasoning and faith before knowledge, as opinion before certitude and the foolishness of God before the wisdom of this world,* it sometimes hesitates and trembles,[8] but not to the point of contradicting. For it is not so much that the reason pulls the will along, but rather the will seems to pull the reason to faith. And it happens, by the enlightenment of grace, that faith begins to grasp the understanding, hope the hunger, and charity the sense of its own good. In the meantime, these bring man to a realization of his weakness so that he may show himself to himself; so that, at the same time, a nature vitiated by sin and exceedingly prone to its

*Eph 3:19

*1 Co 13:12

*1 Co 1:24

physical senses might be freed from the service of the flesh; and that, by the workings of the Holy Spirit, he may through the exertion of piety gradually be conformed to the spiritual and divine reality occupying his thoughts.

This takes great exertion, and no one can accomplish it without the great help of God's grace; this is: to believe and to love, without having taken reason into account and without hesitation, that which is proposed for belief; and by a love of what is to be believed to love believing itself; and to do this to such an extent that the greatness of love takes away the scruple of mistrust, since even in a certain faith—faith can be certain just as long as there is faith—knowledge cannot be certain. It cannot be otherwise than as the Apostle says: Now I know in part.* Anyone who does not accept discipline in this swiftly falls from the pathway of grace and is pulled back onto the path of corrupt nature and becomes an animal man who does not perceive the things of God.* He begins to believe incorrectly, that is, to think incorrectly concerning faith. When the temptor meddles in this person's reflections, he occasionally takes even the faith out of his heart and goes away,* and the last state of this person is worse than the first.* In fact, the enemy attacks especially to vex or to sift the faith in God's servant or, if he can, to destroy it, for he is not unaware that a conscience devoted to God is never more to be grievously dejected or never more seriously saddened once he has turned his face to the face of God. In all this the devotion of his servant possesses the way to God, and the

*1 Co 13:12

*1 Co 2:14.
Cf. Ep frat
XIII, 46-54
et seqq.
(CF 12:27)

*Jn 6:67
*Mt 12:45

consolation or grace of the Lord his God the way to man's heart. From all this there comes to him the incentive of all his own goods; in it is found his only consolation for labors and sorrows.

13. Faith is indeed the first step forward to God. As the Apostle says: It behooves those going to God to believe that he is a rewarder of those seeking him.* Faith is the root of all the powers and the foundation of all good works. Nor is there any power which is not derived from faith. There are no buildings but only ruins outside the foundation of faith. Because of this, the malice of the old serpent began to infect this root first. He is always trying to shake this foundation first, if he can, so that faith will not even exist and, if it does, at least so that it will be imperfect or so that any awareness of illuminating grace may be obscured in it or that the richness of spiritual fulness* may be carried off to himself. Nowadays this blasphemer snake is not even afraid to slither into the paradise of God, to tempt the minds of the faithful, to hiss blasphemies, to cast the spells of various suspicions over the faith. But anyone who has already advanced in the faith should know that it is always better to crush his evil, his head, by despising him rather than by answering him on any single point. If one gets into the habit of speaking with him, the advantage is surely given to his depraved malice, for no one escapes the contagion of deadly poison if he will not remove himself entirely from the pestilence breathed by his venomous mouth.

In mankind there are two temptations, or

*Heb 11:6

*Ps 63:5

weaknesses congealed in nature on account of
the punishment of that very sin: the yearning
of the flesh and blasphemy of the Spirit.
Wherefore, at the very outset, to the first
parents of the human race, the old serpent
hissed the yearning for the forbidden fruit
and blasphemy against God, saying to the
woman: Why has God commanded you not to

Gn 2:1   eat from the tree in the middle of paradise?*
For He knew that from the very day you eat,

Gn 2:5   you will be like gods.* By these words the
gullible woman was easily persuaded that God
was jealous of man. The woman was egged on
by the serpent, and the man by the woman,
into transgressing the divine precept by yearning for the forbidden fruit. Since at that time
all human nature was in them, all human

Rm 5:12   nature sinned.* And from then on, because
of this, the flesh lusts against the spirit and

Gal 5:17   the spirit against the flesh;* and man, bound
Rm 7:14 ff.   under sin, has been rendered impotent,*
often yearning for what he does not want,
often thinking about the things of God in
ways he does not want to, especially with the
incentives of these evils hanging over him, in a
spirit of blasphemy and a spirit of fornication.
Fornication and blasphemy, among all the
pests of temptations, seem to have a special
mark of evil; they threaten with some force
and assail reluctant persons particularly by
the judgment of reason and the exertion of
their reflections. Yet they are quite easily put
to flight by people fleeing away from them
and overcome by people who contemn them.

1 Co 6:18   So the Apostle says: Flee fornication!* For
all memory of this must be put to flight or

utterly contemned lest when circumstances are just right, conscience of the person who is reluctant to do this and who dwells on it be stained, for the natural itch of the flesh is immediately excited by even the lightest touch of reflection.

To the devil who was tempting him to blasphemy and saying: All this I will give you if you will fall down and adore me,* the Doctor of truth opposed only the shield of truth and authority, saying: It is written: You will worship the Lord your God, and him only will you serve.* But in the Book of Kings, when the minions of the Assyrian king blasphemed the Lord, Hezechiah ordered his own, saying: Give them no answer!*   *Mt 4:9*

  Mt 4:10

  Is 36:21 & 2 K 18:36

14. For we must not answer the spirit of blasphemy in any way or converse with it, but only oppose to it the shield of faith. Its virulent malice tries to pollute whatever you bring against it. It does not do this to get a satisfying answer, but is only putting on pressure to sadden the conscience of the believer or somehow to corrupt the purity of his faith.

15. These are twin evils; one is the sting of the flesh, the other that of the soul. Among lazy persons they are both like a natural reminder which takes its origin, as I have said, from the one who yearned to be like God because of the incantation of the old serpent. Immediately given over to the yearnings of the flesh, he blushed at himself and covered those parts of the body which He, who had created them, created without any need for covering. Each vice must have its own antidote. The same remedy does not apply to all

members. What heals the head does not heal the foot, nor can what heals the weakness of the soul heal the weakness of the flesh. Temptation of the flesh needs afflictions of the flesh and physical labors, but temptation of the soul cries out for the help of prayer, reading and meditation and any other spiritual study there may be. In particular one never acquires purity of faith except by true and profound humility of heart, dutiful devotion and unflagging perseverance in prayer. We must pray frequently, therefore, and must say: Lord, increase in us our faith!* Often those who are advancing in it, if they do not have the grace that helps them, suffer a natural uneasiness.

*Lk 17:5

Rationality, I have said, in itself restless and impudent often assaults faith there, where it possesses the faculty of reasoning, although with no intention of contradicting it; not so that it can run against faith but so that it can run with faith. As human reason is accustomed to act in human realities through, as it were, the unavoidable medium of believing, so it tries to break through into the recognition of divine realities. But since it mounts from a different direction, it slips, it stumbles, it sinks until it turns back to the door of faith, to him who said: I am the door.* And once humbled beneath the yoke of divine authority, as it is more humble, so more securely does it enter in.

*Jn 10:9

But there are some persons who never experience temptation: some because of the enormity of their laziness, some because of the torpor of their reason, some because of the certainty of enlightened faith.

16. For the time being, the faith revealed by flesh and blood suffices for the dull-witted and the lazy person. He is not tempted because he is not being examined spiritually.* When someone does not know what faith is, either the habit of assenting or an expression of declared faith is adequate for him. If he were to know, he would certainly apply himself to understanding what he believes.

*1 Co 2:14. See ¶11.

The faith which flesh and blood reveals is one type; another is that which the Father in heaven reveals.* They are not identical. The faith is the same: the effect is different. The one teaches what we must believe, the other prompts understanding of faith, and the full etymology of the understanding, since the person who believes in the *affectus** of his heart stands under what he believes.† The one is the teacher, the tutor or author of human infirmities; but the other is the very inheritance and perfection of liberty. The one tolerates lazy persons, nor does it exclude dull-witted persons, holding out to everyone the outlines of truth. The other receives only those who are fervent in spirit, serving the Lord and having the eyes of their heart enlightened.*

*Mt 16:17

*See backnote 6.
†Literally: reads into—intus legit ⇒intelligit.

*Rm 12:11, Eph 1:18

We are not calling dull-witted those simple sons of God with whom He has frequent communication,* whose unique merit and singular grace is that they deserve to receive the faith by God's revelation—not only is it the faith which flesh and blood reveals but also that which the Father who is in heaven reveals. Those who are taught by God* learn from the Holy Spirit apart from the racket of

*Pr 3:32

*Jn 6:45

argumentative words or reflections. If the Spirit is not himself present in the teacher and disciple in this kind of teaching, the noisy reasonings of reason fail. For these are not lazy persons; they are simple and uniquely strong and prudent in faith. Nor in their silence are they to be considered dull-witted, rather they are wise in what they have uniquely accepted, because they have sensed the Lord in goodness,* and they sense with a sense of love* whatever they believe about God. They savor what they sense and when reasonings tire and drop out they keep running, for they walk simply, they walk confidently.* For [they trust] not in the chariots of their own cleverness or in the horses of human self-reliance but in the name of the Lord;* not in book-learning, but in the powers of the Lord and in his justice alone.* For they make no distinctions in faith, they analyze nothing. Continually offering every judgment of their own reason to be enlightened by the Holy Spirit and directing their every sense to assent in faith, they sweetly and confidently seize its spiritual fruit. And they sense something of the Lord in goodness, for they seek him in simplicity of heart. And he is found by them, for they do not tempt him. He appears to them because they have faith in him.* There is fulfilled in them what the Lord Jesus, praying to the Father for the disciples, said: And truly these have known that I have come forth from you.* How have they known? It continues: And they have believed that you sent me.* Yes, they have really known for they have really believed.

*Ws 1:1

*See ¶21 below & backnote 11.

*Pr 10:9

*Ps 20:7

*Ps 71:15-16

*Ws 1:1-2

*Jn 17:8

*Ibid.

There are persons who are dull-witted about their faith, who naturally do not understand or who are not able to understand; for others it is too much trouble to work hard at acquiring the ability to understand although they could.

By no means are we extolling the simple person simply believing as if to discredit a person of spiritual discernment;* someone who, if he is not a scrutinizer of majesty,* is yet an admirer of piety and imitator of simplicity. Not only does he evade the enticing snares of temptation but, learning from them, he also progresses magnificently. Their graces are different.

*1 Co 2:14
*Pr 25:27

17. It is one thing to have simple faith and to grasp the sweetness of its fruit simply in the heart; it is another thing to understand what one believes and always to be prepared to render a reason for one's faith. Simple faith savors but gives no light and is more removed from temptations. But the other type, although it savors with effort, gives light and is safer against temptations. While one advances step by step in the faith, bearing Christ dwelling within his heart by faith, he possesses a sure knowledge of the various matters of faith, as his conscience acclaims. And he fosters that faith which flesh and blood reveal to him with a very fervent embrace and aspires to it. When it is given to him, he relaxes sweetly in what his Father who is in heaven reveals. And although he is often overtaken by the simple man who is using the shortcut of his devout simplicity, he is nevertheless not held back from the fountain of grace which is open to

all. Working in sorrows, in the thorns and
nettles of his earth, amid the temptations of
his corrupt nature, by the sweat of his brow
ever since Adam's curse, he eats his own
Gn 3:17   bread. Sometimes, although he does not
know it, he, like Jacob, finds the blessings of
Gn 27:27   the Lord in the meadow of his heart. For
the effort of spiritual exertion, expended
faithfully in faith, cannot be useless, nor can
the sorrow of this interval, dutifully measured
out, be cheated of its reward.

Illuminating grace is often present to a
struggling faith and thus, as by the thrust of a
lance, brings to it a recognition of and hope
for things invisible, and in that recognition
and hope, love; until without any space of
intervening time and shift of sense the love
coming from faith, by the mediation of hope,
continuously rises through recognition. And
faith too is integrated in love through recognition to such an extent, as I have already said
above, that the recognition of faith and hope
and love (although these three are understood
to be distinct in that very faith, still, in the
power of that very faith, by some argument
of affinity they) become, in the sense of the
person who believes, one, the indivisible substance of things hoped for. This is when what
we believe, we recognize by believing; but
what we really recognize, we hope for because
we recognize its good, and we love what we
know and hope for. What he believes and
hopes for and loves ought always to be present to the faithful soul in love, and yet he
cannot always have it in his understanding.

These are the special powers of the soul in

which all her strength consists. These are the bones which the psalmist very often calls to mind: the Lord guards them in his saints.* *Ps 34:19-20 When they are joined to one another, there is made from them one bone which is not broken.* This is the perfection of faith in this *Ex 12:45, Nb 9:12, Jn 19:36 life; of it is said elsewhere: my bone, which you have made in secret, is not hidden from you.* Yet, separated from one another, they *Ps 139:15 are easily disturbed and greatly disturb the soul;* they are either shattered—and our *Ps 6:3-4 enemies reproach us*—or they are scattered— *Ps 42:10 and make a worse hell for us.* When our *Ps 141:7 flesh, that is, the other affections of our soul, adheres to them and their strength comes from the bones and the bones draw from them in return the moisture of a healthy fatness, *eucrasis* comes about, that is, a well-composed soul.* If they are separated from *William develops this idea of eucrasis in Nat corp; PL 180:697A (CF 24:106). one another, the flesh dries up and the bones begin to die, both wasting away in themselves. So faith without works, hope without the consolation of increase, charity without the tenderness of piety [all] dry up like tinder.* *Ps 102:4 When the flesh adheres to the bones, therefore, it is good for the flesh and for the bones because the flesh becomes more solid from the strength of the bones and the bones are nourished by the flesh. But if the bone adheres to the flesh as the prophet deplores in a certain place, saying: My bones have adhered to my flesh,* it softens into flesh and *Ps 102:5 is made completely flesh. This means: if the affections of the soul conform to faith, man lives in the spirit and walks in the spirit; he is, as it were, wholly spirit.* But if these *Gal 5:25

spiritual powers are relaxed into physical affections, the whole becomes flesh and it is said
of that man: my spirit will not remain in this
man for he is flesh.*

*Gn 6:3

18.   Faith must be nourished with its own
food, therefore, for the person being examined spiritually.* Before all else, God must
affect it† with the spirit of humility until
that substance of things hoped for* begins to
appear in ardent devotion, so that, as I have
said already, the fervor of natural reasoning
may be transformed by the workings of grace
into the fervor of love, importunate reasoning
may be turned into love's contemplation, and
the knowledge of what is discovered into the
joy of fulfillment. But in the meantime, while
nature is being both exercised and educated
and taught what it is capable of without
grace, even though we hold back by reason
the natural fervor of rationality lest it boil
over into contradiction, we can scarcely bring
it to pass that something boiling does not boil!
The result is that our natural appetite for
knowledge does not always seriously consider
believing what it is not allowed to probe into
for the purpose of analysis by one of its
senses either of the reason or of the body.

*See above
¶ ¶11 & 16.
†See Appendix.
*Heb 11:1

But do not fear, servant of God. Do not move
your feet, do not waste your steps!* Infidels
seek signs, the hesitant require wisdom.* But
you, embrace Christ Crucified, a stumbling
block to those predestined to ruin, foolishness
to those who are wise in their own eyes, but to
all those who are called and justified the wisdom of God and the power of God, for the
foolishness of God is wiser and his weakness is

*Ps 73:2
*1 Co 1:22

stronger than all men.* If you consult the
sense of the flesh, it seems foolish and weak.*
Yet if, with the Apostle,* you have the sense
of Christ, you will understand that the Word
of God is the supreme wisdom but the foolishness of this wisdom is the flesh of the Word.
This is so that those who are carnal, who are
not able through the prudence of the flesh
to attain to the wisdom of God, may be
healed through the foolishness of preaching*
and simplicity of faith, that is, through the
flesh of the Word. Be foolish that you may be
wise,* and there will be lighted up for you the
economy of the mystery hidden for all ages in
God who created every creature. Be as weak as
God's weakness and you will learn how
exceedingly great is the greatness of his
power in [those of] us who have believed,
according to the workings of the force of his
power.*

19. A momentary and fleeting confusion
over what she believes should not frighten the
faithful soul. There is in her no lack of good
conscience about her faith nor, in this conscience, witness of the Holy Spirit, even if the
interrogation is made during an examination for
martyrdom. O faithful soul, innocent nature
does not damn you, but it boggles at anything
unfamiliar; it does not draw away but draws
back. Sometimes it believes; but sometimes it
seeks to know.[9]

Consider the Mother of the Lord, a special
sign of faith. Once she had received the good
news of our salvation and of her conceiving
by the seal of the Holy Spirit, she believed
with absolute certainty that she would be

*1 Co 1:23-25
*Col 2:18
*1 Co 2:16

*1 Co 1:22

*1 Co 3:18

*Eph 1:19

the Mother of the Lord. Nevertheless, there was something she wanted to know, the manner of fulfilling this mystery. She asked:

Lk 1:34 How shall this be for I do not know a man?* She held the reality by faith, but she wanted to know the manner. Her faithful soul embraced the reality, comforted by the very grace of which she was full; but her nature, astonished, was wondering at the manner by which it would happen. She was already feeling within herself the Holy Spirit operating in a unique way, but she did not know how he would accomplish in her flesh without the help of flesh the wonderful things she believed. The angel said to her: The Spirit of the Most High will come upon you, and the Power

Lk 1:35 of the Most High will overshadow you.* It is
Ex 8:19 as if he said: The finger of God is here.* So too, concerning the spiritual regeneration of baptism, the Lord replied to Nicodemus who wanted to know the manner [of regeneration]: The Spirit breathes where he wills, and you hear his voice, and you know not where he comes from and where he goes. Thus

Jn 3:8 is everyone who is born of the Spirit.* To those fretting about the sacramental mystery of his Body and Blood he says: It is the Spirit who gives life; the flesh, however, does not

Jn 6:64 profit anyone.* For one and the same Spirit
1 Co 12:11 does all this as he wills,* so constituting the sacraments of faith that some of them are the corporal and visible signs of the sacred reality —as in baptism and in the sacrament of the Body and Blood of the Lord—and that others are only sacred things concealed and open to investigation by a spiritual understanding

guided by the Holy Spirit himself. Of these last the Apostle says: That he might make known to you the mystery of his will.*   *Eph 1:9*

CHAPTER TEN

Faith in the Sacraments
and Mysteries of Religion

THE WILL OF GOD is the hidden and highest mystery of all the sacraments which he makes known according to his good pleasure to whom he chooses and as he chooses, [a mystery] which, because it is divine, in some divine manner he then reveals to the person who is worthy in the process making him worthy. Better yet, it is not divine, it is God, for it is the Holy Spirit, who is the substantial will of God. This is the Will of God whereby God makes all that he wills, about whom it is written: Everything that the Lord willed he did.* The same Holy Spirit, then, makes himself known to the person into whom he pours himself. The very Will of God makes himself known to the person in whom it is accomplished; nor is it known anywhere other than where he is. Even if the eye of human reason cannot hide itself from the brightness of his light and truth, only the person who does this [will] can be a partaker of His sweetness and only by willing what God wills. Just as a person does not sense unless he is alive, because the life by which one senses is only present in a living creature, so no one

*Ps 135:6

knows [His Will] in whom it is not accomplished, although not everyone knows it or senses it in some persons where it is, for example, in infants and the feebleminded.

20. Just as there are many persons who have a soul and do not know what a soul is, so there are many who have grace but do not know what it is. To the person on whom it exerts an influence, it reveals the external sacraments when the very reality signified in all the sacraments is working in him. It is the Holy Spirit himself who sanctifies externals so that they may be the sacraments of so great a reality. By revealing them, he commends them to the faithful conscience in whom the hidden grace effects the reality of the sacrament. God is more intimate to us than our inmost being;* for our outer being, that is, the senses of the body, he establishes for us the external sacraments through which he would lead our inmost being to his inmost being. Through the workings of the physical sacraments he gradually excites in us spiritual grace. It is for this purpose that he humbled himself to fellowship with our humanity: that he might make us partakers of his divinity.*

*Augustine, Conf. III, 6

*2 P 1:4

21. As the author of our salvation had commanded, therefore, our flesh is washed outwardly in the waters of baptism; inwardly, the soul is purified by the operation of the Holy Spirit. And thus justified in the faith of the Son of man and the Son of God, sinful men are made the sons of God. The faithful man eats physically but incorruptibly the physical but incorruptible food of the Body and Blood of the Lord: [he eats] physically

as much as corresponds to us, incorruptibly as
much as he raises up, [he eats] what conforms
him to God through the sense of understanding reason, and through the sense of enlightened love [he eats] what unites him to
God. Accustomed to temporal things, we
must be cleansed by temporal things. And
once cleansed, we shall not be worthy of
contemplation of the eternal unless, in the
process of being purified by temporal things,
we have summoned forth faith. These things
are indeed temporal and transitory, but
Rm 8:23 through the first fruits of the Spirit,* they
nevertheless bear the first fruits of things
eternal. Both are consistent with professing
the faith and implementing the truth, to our
mortality and to the eternity to come. This is
most compellingly obvious to us in the person
of the Mediator who, remaining in himself
eternal God, has been made man in time that
through him, temporal and eternal, we may
pass from things temporal to the eternal. Consequently, as I have said, we eat the Body of
the Lord and drink his Blood physically, but
we are refreshed spiritually. We are washed
physically in baptism but we are purified
spiritually. The assent of our faith has been
being taught, step by step, by these rudiments
of christian piety. When we do not tempt the
Lord our God in this [assent], but simply
Credere: to believe and faithfully confide* our spirit to him, he
and to confide. also begins to confide himself to us, so that
we may be no longer among those about
whom one reads in the gospels that they
believed in Jesus but he did not believe in
Jn 2:23-24 them.* It has been said of them, incorrectly,

that they believed in him whom they did not
love. But to believe in him is to go to him by
loving him. They believe that he was the Christ,
but they did not love him as the Christ. He did
not confide himself to those to whose inward
eye he did not appear in that form in which he
cannot not be loved by anyone who can see him.[10]

First of all in the realities of God, therefore,
we are obliged to give the simple and pure
assent of faith without any wavering or hesitation. Then, to understand what we believe,
along with observing and obeying the com-
mands of God, we are obliged to confide to
the Holy Spirit all our spirit and understanding. This is not so much an attempt of the
scope of reason as the affection of simple and
devout love. And so, by the serious application of an absolutely humble piety rather than
by the force of a capable ingenuity, we shall
deserve to have Jesus begin to confide himself to us. With grace illuminating the understanding of reason, the assent of faith will be
changed into the sense of love,[11] to recognize
inwardly the sacrament of the will of God.
[This sense of love] no longer needs the external sacraments. Yet as long as we live here
below our outward being is bound up with
their most holy bonds and through them our
inmost being, lest it trickle out to alien things.
Wherefore, religion derives its name from
this 'binding'.[12]

22. Placed in the body, we have been confined and contained by the corporal forms of
the sacraments and by obedience to the
wisdom of God who instituted them. We are
confronted with the physical forms of the

CHAPTER ELEVEN

Proper Dispositions for Faith

THE UNCLEAN SOUL, the impure consciousness, the proud mind, curious con-
ceit, is moreover, rightly kept at a
distance from the quest of the divine sacraments and mysteries, for the spirit of discipline flees anything false and will not dwell in
a body subject to sin. And wisdom will not
enter into an ill-disposed soul.*   *Ws 1:4-5

But humble piety, believing love, and a pure
conscience, the simple sons of God and the
poor in spirit, although they reverently withdraw, are called forward by the Holy Spirit,
and in a special sort of way are drawn to
inquire into these things. For they love and
therefore they seek when they do seek, and
they seek to love still more.

Consequently, O faithful soul, when in your
faith the more hidden mysteries impinge on
your timorous nature, be brave and say, not
in an attempt to stave them off but in a love
of following them: How can these things
be?* Let your question be your prayer, let it   *Lk 1:34
be your love and your humble desire, not
considering the majesty of God in lofty
matters but seeking salvation in the saving
acts of the God of our salvation.* And the   *Ps 68:20

53

angel of mighty council will reply to you:
When the Paraclete shall come whom I will
send you from the Father, he will bear witness
of me and will bring all things to your mind,
and the Spirit of truth will teach you all

*Jn 14:26; 15:26;
  16:13

truth.* As no one knows those things that are
of man, except the spirit which is in him, so
no one knows those things of God except the

*1 Co 2:11

Spirit of God.* Hasten to be partakers of the
Holy Spirit then, He is present when he is
invoked and he will not help unless he is
invoked. When invoked, he comes; he comes

*Rm 15:29

in the abundance of God's blessing.* He is the
torrent of the river making happy the city of

*Ps 46:4

God.* And if, when he shall come, he finds
you humble and quiet and fearing the words

*Is 66:2

of God,* he will rest upon you and he will
reveal to you what God the Father withdraws

*Mt 11:25

from the wise and prudent of this world.*
Those things which Wisdom was able to teach
the disciples on earth will begin to enlighten
you. But they could not bear it until the
Spirit of Truth came, who taught them all

*Jn 16:12-13

truth.* In such perceiving or learning, it is
futile to expect from the mouth of any man at
all what could not be perceived or learned
from the tongue of Truth itself. For as Truth

*Jn 4:24

himself has said: God is spirit.*

23. And just as it is necessary that those
who worship him worship him in spirit and in

*Ibid.

truth,* so it behooves those wanting to know
and understand him to seek the understanding
of faith, the sense of that pure and undivided
truth, only in the Holy Spirit. For in the darkness and ignorance of this life he is himself
the light that enlightens the poor in spirit. He

is the charity that draws them. He is the sweetness that *affects** them, he is man's access to God; he is the love of the lover; he is devotion; he is piety; he reveals to the faithful from faith in faith the justice of God, because he gives grace for grace,* and to the faith of the hearer, the faith that enlightens.

*I.e., touches them deeply. See Appendix.

*Jn 1:16

As the Apostle says, there are those who have piety of some kind indeed, but deny power.* Surely there is present to all men that form of faith which can be given to men only by men through the words and institutions of ecclesiastical discipline, in the assent of good will. Since man still sees in a mirror and in an enigma*[13] and passes like an image,* it is in a mirror that we are taught by metaphor, and it is by a yet more obscure enigma that we are trained, in the simple and evident image that we are more sweetly affected.* Yet, piety itself, truth itself, is given or taught only by the Holy Spirit! Only by the finger of God is it inscribed on the mind.

*2 Tm 3:5

*1 Co 13:12
*Ps 39:6

*See Appendix.

CHAPTER TWELVE

The Proper Object of Faith

UNHESITATINGLY believe that the Holy Trinity, Father, Son and Holy Spirit, of one substance, has with an inseparable equality a divine unity, and also that there are not three gods but one God. Believe that God, made man for us, the best medicine to heal the tumor of our pride, the profound sacrament for our redemption and the forgiveness of our sins, has performed miracles and has risen from the dead. If you know what omnipotence is, believe of the Omnipotent that he could do it. If you are sensitive to what the supreme good is, the supreme goodness when the need of the lost was so dire, believe of the supreme good that he willed it. If you can reflect on what divinity, humbled, brought about in the world, be sensitive of the Lord in his good- *Ws 1:1* ness* how becoming to its God was this activity. First, in the cause of human salva- tion the Father did not spare the Son nor the Son himself. In his form the supreme good was manifested in the world and he taught man how to love God as he ought to be loved. Loving man to the extent even of despising Himself, He taught man how to love God to the contempt of himself; man who, poor wretch, only knew how to love himself even to the contempt of God.

And this is piety; this is the proper adoration of God* by which God ought to be adored by his creature. This is the wisdom which Supreme Wisdom brings into the world, creating in it so many glorious martyrs, so many persons perfect in contemning themselves and the world. This is the wisdom of God, proper to the person who is sensitive to God, to the one who lives by the spirit of His life* to the point of sensing His love, to the one who loves to the point of imitating His likeness; proper in temporal things to the person who feels in himself what was also in Christ Jesus our Lord,* but proper in eternal things in respect to God, having that sense about which a certain wise man says: To know you is this sense raised to perfection.* In the form of the mediator shines forth uniquely that long-established definition of wisdom:* the recognition of things human and divine, so that one may understand or be more and more sensitive until, as I have said, one comes to savor loving, until one comes to the *affectus*[14] of imitating Our Lord Jesus Christ who although he was in the form of God did not think it robbery to make himself equal to God when he humbled himself, taking the form of a slave even to the point of dying on the cross. Who, what, for whom did he do this?*

In remembering, understanding and loving, one is made similar to Supreme Wisdom and becomes wise in God. Because of this, he

*Augustine, The Trinity, XII, 14.

*Rm 8:2, Gal 5:25

*Ph 2:5

*Ws 6:16 (LXX)

*Augustine, Against the Academicians, I,vi,16; The Trinity 14.11, 14,1.3; Seneca Ep 89:4; Isidore, Etymologies 20.8.6; Abelard, Christian Theology II,39, inter alia.

*Ph 2:6-8

draws out some wisdom by adoring God as
God. By it he seasons his life, his manners and
his actions and all other things with a sort of
divine savor on behalf of all men and anoints
them with a kind of oil of gladdening grace so
that all men, seeing his good works, may glorify his Father who is in heaven.* He has grace
towards his friends, patience with kindness
towards his enemies. He can give kindness to
anyone he wants to; he is utterly well-
disposed to all persons; and he holds to that
natural law,* whereby no one wants to do
what he does not want done to himself, but
insofar as he can does for everyone else what
he wants done to himself.

24. Moreover, Wisdom sets apart in its
wise subject a knowledge [derived] from this
wisdom, not the kind that seeks the vain
things of this world but the kind that serves
the faith in which we stand and are glorified
in the hope of the glory of God's sons.*
This knowledge is a sort of quality or habit
of the mind for receiving those things which
are unique to faith, those things, that is,
which are sensibly brought into the mind
through its own or others' senses, either by
the person himself who senses or by another
who speaks or writes. Such things are the
temporal deeds of the Lord's life recognized
in their historical dimension: his nativity,
passion, resurrection, ascension and his miracles performed among men. Man's reason does
not come to recognize them wholly within
himself, as he does discover certain divine and
eternal truths, but he accepts them by a particular way of learning either by seeing or

*Mt 5:16

*Augustine,
Commentary
on Ps. LVII, 1.

*Rm 5:2

hearing or reading, as it were, coming from without.

To the mind created for eternity, that it might through its intelligence be capable of and by its enjoyment might share in it, things human and eternal seemed joined, as if by some natural affinity, to such an extent that although it may become quite blunted on account of its weakness, it still never loses its hunger for them. Although it may not be able to recognize invisible things well, its powers of recognition are nevertheless so solidly joined to human reason that it can never at any time draw away from the good and the beautiful, from its love of or delight in blessedness and changelessness except when, in its hunger for or its love of good, it is deceived by a false good. Even if nature has from creating grace, a hunger for these things still it cannot tell them apart perfectly except by illuminating grace, nor does it apprehend them unless God grants this.

25. Therefore, when one who is converted to the Lord* remembers, he easily finds what is known of God* naturally sinking into his mind or reason. These temporal things are discerned temporally, introduced as it were into the soul through the senses. They do not easily adhere in the mind until, by increasing faith and illuminating grace, the knowledge of these temporal things is transformed into the wisdom of things eternal and the realities of time are clothed with the grace of eternity, when Christ Jesus begins not only to be perceived according to the flesh* but to be understood according to his deeds and

*Ps 22:27
*Rm 1:19

*2 Co 5:16

esteemed according to his works. According to the Prophet who says: They have announced the works of God and they have understood his deeds,* it is no great thing to announce the works of God if his deeds are not understood. For all the deeds of the Word are words to us by which he speaks to us, showing himself to us in deeds of his [which are] correctly understood. They are understood not only through mystical interpretations in the reflections and in the utterances of knowledge but much more sweetly and effectively through the affections of devout love, in meditation or the utterance of wisdom. This is what the Apostle says: To some is given the uttering of wisdom through the Spirit, to others the uttering of knowledge.* But meanwhile, until Christ is formed in us, faith, because it is a thing of knowledge, naturally, as it were, hungers to know anything that is set out to it to be believed. When it cannot do this, it becomes agitated.

*Ps 64:9

*1 Co 12:18

CHAPTER THIRTEEN

Degrees of Understanding

THIS KNOWLEDGE or manner of receiving those truths of faith means that supreme wisdom arranged all things in the conscience of the person accepting them. First, out of obedience to the Lord who says: Anyone who has believed, will be saved, but anyone who has not believed will be condemned,* an hospitable grace, as it were, is not refused those things which, as I have said, come from outside, by a simple assent [sprung] from obedience to the one who enjoins them. But later they are received through the intimacy of a good will, as in civil law and the fellowship of social life, in the communion of the same bread and chalice. Still later, the *affectuses*[15] are joined as if by a mutual marriage when the intelligible things understood by the senses and the sensible things understood by the intelligence commend themselves to one another; when they confer reciprocally on one another those things in which they abound; and when temporal things commend God and make intelligible the omnipotent goodness of God, they

Mk 16:16

61

endow the faith dependent on temporal things with the goodness and power of the Lord because, being good, he willed, and, being powerful, he was able to act for, human salvation—a thing human nature can hardly believe.

The invisible things of God in this especially are seen by understanding those things which *Rm 1:20* have been made,* since the temporal dispensation of the Mediator—believed correctly through faith or through that knowledge which comes of faith—teaches and nourishes the heart of the believer so that he may grasp eternal truths. And the eternal truths, once correctly recognized, make the testimony of *Ps 93:5* the temporal things extremely credible.* The dignity of the work testified in the heart of the person who understands to the greatness of divine goodness, and the supreme good, understood to some degree by the sense of *See backnote n. 11.* love,* constitute a work worthy of God. In all this, the supreme wisdom enlightened us concerning the kingdom of charity that exists in the state of eternity, to the measure of his gift yet beyond the measure of our grasp, when he who was in the form of God, [yet] *Ph 2:6-9* made in the form of a servant,* taught those who could understand through the things which he did what good is waiting for us in the realm of the supreme good. This was done in time but in him who was in the beginning *Jn 1:1-4* with God.* His life was his work, and he was eternally with God. From him a new wisdom has flowed out into the world, a wisdom above all the wisdom of this world and making *1 Co 1:20* it foolishness.* For those who understand and

savor them, the weak and foolish things of
God are wiser and stronger than the things of
all men*—for those who savor with a tender   *1 Co 1:25*
savor of mind the humility of the Son of God
to the point of death, even the death on a
cross,* the passion of the one who suffered   *Ph 2:8*
for us, the mockery, blows, spittle, scourging,
thorns and nails, and all the rest. Any soul
wounded by charity is sometimes scarcely
able to recall all this, so heavy is her sorrow,
yet the *affectus* of love[16] will never allow her
to forget it. Because of this, the temporal
deeds of the Lord become in the believing
heart both the wonderful sacraments of eternity and a wondrous incentive to imitate
the same sufferings until, loving as much as it
can, human weakness burns to love more than
it can and to suffer for him more than frail
humanity can suffer. This happens when,
according to the precept of the Apostle, the
faithful man sanctifies the Lord Jesus in his
heart* and the Lord Jesus sanctifies himself   *1 P 3:15*
in him.*   *Jn 17:19*

CHAPTER FOURTEEN

The Various Aides to Faith

IF ONLY everyone who professes this faith would live it to the full! May everyone who has it glory in being numbered among the ranks of the faithful. No one should entertain the opinion that one can have this faith toward God who still appears to be keeping faith with this world. For this reason the Apostle says: Those who thrust off a good conscience have made shipwreck of their faith.* A bad conscience easily suffers the shipwreck of its faith. Persons who have a mind corrupted by a yearning for the world and the flesh conduct themselves neither honestly nor honorably in regard to faith. For this reason the Apostle also says about them: They are corrupt in mind, dishonest about their faith.* Yet one's whole nature is instantly stunned at the slightest wounding of the heart or brain or those parts in the body in which life is contained, so too, if one is truly faithful, at the very faintest pulse of faith, the entire substance of a good will trembles. And as the serpent's prudence accustoms it to expose its whole body to defend its head, in which its life is contained, so the faithful man refuses to do or to suffer

*1 Tm 1:19

*2 Tm 3:8

nothing as long as the health of his faith remains undisturbed.

We must therefore assiduously pray to Our Father who is in heaven* that even if he allows our faith, in being tested, to be led into temptation, he will not allow it to endure temptation to the point of condemnation* but will offer with the temptation such growth that we may sustain it.* The help of grace must be sought with complete seriousness of piety against the sense of the flesh and the fervor of nature, lest faith fall apart, lest it fail. May it instead bear fruit in patience* until, little by little, the grace of the Holy Spirit exalts that whole effigy of quaking nature into the substance of perfect faith, perfecting in it David's prayer: Take away my opprobrium which I have dreaded.* Let the prudent mind appropriate to itself for building up its faith, for confirming its heart,* for enlightening the conscience of faith, the great lights of the Church, the men greatest in spiritual knowledge, in supreme wisdom, in proven holiness, and their doctrines and writing, their works and martyrdoms. Let him say to himself against the movements of his own temptations: Are you really better than they are, holier, wiser, sharper, than those who have taught the world what they learned from the Lord? They preached it magnificently. They have handed down to us rich descriptions [of it] ; they have confirmed it by their lives and miracles and have made it holy by their deaths and martyrdoms.

These kinds of thoughts about faith and fluctuations of the mind and hesitations of

*Mt 6:9

*Mt 6:13

*1 Co 10:13

*Lk 8:15

*Ps 119:39

*1 Th 3:13

reflections swirl mostly around the humanity of the Saviour and those mysteries of faith which are revealed to us in it. Whether it comes from God, or whether all things created and established through its omnipotence are done through his providence, these truths concerning the supreme essence so demonstrate themselves and make themselves manifest to every conscience capable of reason that there is not one person who does not understand that his existence has come from God, if he knows about himself what he really is. This is so true that not even the fool dares to say in his heart: There is no God,* meaning [there is no God] in a foolish and silly heart. In no single person who is in his right mind is there to be found such human depravity that he does not know God is the Creator of every creature, [God] who is above every creature insofar as every creature comes from him. He is beyond all time, for with him there is no time. He is beyond all place for with him there is no place. He, the changeless one, changes all things. Immovable, he moves all things. Utterly the source of all things, of all change and of all motion, he must be considered, without doubt, the immovable power and rational cause of all things both created and moved.

26. Since from eternity he has predestined with fixed and immovable causes all things which shall come to be, he has, according to the prophet, already done all future things.* To think frankly about all these things referring to God is proper to few persons, although it pertains to the human

*Ps 14:1; 53:1;
Augustine,
Comm. on
Psalm LII, 2.

*Qo 3:15

nature which every rational man has within himself. Because of this, truth, even when not known, is loved by all men, rooted as it is in the image of supreme truth and supreme good. When what one believes and understands is good, one hungers for eternity and loves incorruptibility. If anyone has put the question to himself, therefore, he will quickly find entirely within himself that with which to subdue turbulent reasoning; or accusing himself of slow-wittedness, he will venerate the hidden truth.

We are not able to teach or to learn from man or through man anything concerning the humanity of the Saviour except: He who believes will be saved; he who has not believed will be condemned.* There are here many and manifold—and in this case, very appropriate— reasons why God both could and should have done what the gospel preaching affirms. That he has done this, what reasons—beyond the gospel authority which carries great weight for and is highly regarded by devout ears and minds—do we adduce for infidels and persons who hesitate? As they say with their mouth or murmur in their hearts, they have seen neither Him nor the works of Him who says: If you do not believe me, then believe my works.* They have not seen the Apostles working miracles in his name or the persons who through them believed the signs that followed, concerning which [the Evangelist] says: These signs will follow those who believe.* Although even today miracles and signs both public and private are not lacking in the Church of God, yet they are performed

*Mk 16:16

*Jn 10:38

*Mk 16:17

in their own places and at their own times and
not at the pleasure of hesitant persons or [to
answer] the questions of the incredulous, but
rather to help the faithful and to console those
working for or in the faith. These signs and
miracles are performed either in them or
through them, not that they may believe but
because they believe.

Yet unbelievers love to err. They have loves
which they do not want to master, and
through them they are sent into error from
which they do not know how to return. The
sense of the flesh is in the persons who do not
know how to think about spiritual things except in a physical way, much less do they
know or can they think about those things
which concern the human dispensation in the
Lord Jesus Christ except carnally.

Unless the Holy Spirit helps the weakness
of the faithful person who seeks devoutly,
asks humbly, knocks religiously, it is much
easier for that person to sense divine things
about God than to reflect on either the divine
things in man or the human things in God;
until, with the Spirit himself helping and
the Lord Jesus Christ sanctifying himself in
the hearts of the faithful by an enlightened
faith, there begins to appear in the one and
same person of the Mediator both the divinity
which makes the humanity clear by its
majesty and the humanity which, in its humility, makes the divinity clear. This is so that
there may be accomplished in these persons
what the Lord himself once said when he was
praying for his disciples: Now is the Son of
Man made clear[17] and God made clear in him.

If God is made clear in him, then God makes
him clear in himself.*   According to the   *Jn 13:31*
manner or progress of the interior purity of
the hearts of believers, Christ is made clear in
the beauty of his glorified humanity and he
appears in the glory of his divinity in the
affectus of persons of devout faith.[18]

It is not everyone's place nor is there
granted everyone in this life what, by a
special privilege of grace, the Lord in the
gospel promises to some, when he says: Some
of those standing here will not taste death
until they see the Son of Man in his kingdom.*   *Mt 16:28*
Stephen saw him in one way at his moment
of martyrdom when, looking intently to
heaven, he saw the heavens open and Jesus
standing at the right hand of the Father.*   *Ac 7:55*
The woman to whom after his resurrection he
said: Do not touch me for I have not yet
ascended to my Father,* saw him in another   *Jn 20:17*
way. Those who are alone with themselves are
likewise made worthy of seeing in yet another
way, by reflecting through faith; in another
way is he in them through the grace that
affects and they in him through the *affectus*
of devotion.[19a]

CHAPTER FIFTEEN

The Goal of the Life of Faith

*2 Co 3:18,
Ps 42:3

*Col 1:15

*Heb 1:3

*2 Co 3:18

WHEN THE SOUL, thirsting for the living God, looks at the glory of God,* then, led by grace, she runs up against the Mediator of God and man, the God-Man Jesus Christ, the Image of the invisible God.* Because of the magnitude of the goodness whereby he was made man for us and of the power of the majesty whereby he is God, [the soul] senses in herself the splendor of God's grace and she becomes what the Apostle calls the figure of his substance.* He says: We, looking at the glory of God with face unveiled, are transformed into that same image from glory to glory as by the spirit of the Lord.* She loves and her love is her sense whereby she senses him whom she senses; and she is somehow transformed into what she senses, for she does not sense him unless she is transformed into him, that is, unless he is in her and she in him.

27. As the outer senses of the body concern themselves with bodily things, so does the inner [sense] with inward realities, that is, with rational and divine or spiritual things. But the inward sense of the soul is its understanding. Yet, a greater and worthier sense

and a purer understanding of the soul is love,
if love is pure. For by this sense the Creator
himself is sensed by the creature; by this
understanding he is understood insofar as
God can be experienced or understood by a
creature.* The sense or the soul of a man,   *See backnote 11.*
when it undertakes to sense, is by this sens-
ing changed into what it senses. Otherwise, it
is not a sense. It is thought, as physicians
assert, that the power of seeing, having gone
out from the brain through the rays of the
eyes, runs up against the forms or colors of
visible things. When it reports them back to
the mind, the mind conforms itself to them,
and vision results. Otherwise, a person seeing
does not see. This must be understood as well
in regard to the other senses. Similarly, the
mind has the understanding for its sense; by
it [the mind] senses whatever it senses. When
it senses things rational, reason goes out to
them, and once it has returned, the mind is
transformed to these realities and understanding occurs. But in those things which pertain
to God, the sense of the mind is love. By this
it senses whatever it senses of God, according
to the spirit of life.* And, the spirit of life is   *Rv 11:11*
the Holy Spirit; by him anyone loves who
loves what truly ought to be loved.

28. For since nothing is loved unless it is
good or is thought to be good, it is given to be
understood that every love and all love is due
only to the supreme good. And it always
returns to It if it is not held bound or captive
elsewhere, where it is deceived by a false good.

29. But the love of God is to our love, to
our natural affection, what our soul is to its

body. If the soul is in it, the body is alive. If not, then it is a carcass and does not sense what it ought to be sensing. When a person is alive and senses through love what ought to be sensed, he is transformed into what he senses, even more effectually by the *affectus*[19b] of a loving person than by the senses into physical things or by the understanding in rational things, and the person is made one spirit with God to whom he is attracted.*

1 Co 6:17

The will of the soul has such force to join even physical realities that in conducting them by the senses it sometimes retains the very sense-impression formed in them with such intensity that the will itself is made love or cupidity or lust.* It regards with such fervent eagerness of intensity the realities sensed that by them it affixes or stains the very body of the person longing eagerly or lovingly until it sometimes transforms it into a like species or color. This did not escape the Patriarch Jacob who employed a natural strategy and an artificial one to impart the colors he wanted to his animals about to be born, lest he be defrauded by the wickedness of a barbarian of his wages for his work.*

Augustine, Trinity, XI, 2, 5.

Gn 30:25-43

30. This process happens in a more forceful and more worthy manner when he, the Holy Spirit, who is the substantial will of the Father and the Son, so attaches the will of a person to Himself that the soul, loving God and, by loving, sensing Him, will be unexpectedly and entirely transformed, not into the nature of divinity certainly, but into a kind of blessedness beyond the human form yet short of the divine, in the joy of

illuminating grace and the sense of an enlightened conscience. This is so true that the spirit
of man which before had scarcely been able
to say in the Holy Spirit: Jesus is Lord,* *1 Co 12:3*
now, amid the sons by adoption, cries out:
Abba, Father!* And not only his spirit but *Rm 8:15*
also his flesh, sensing already the first fruits
of the promised incorruption and glorifica-
tion,* will renounce itself joyfully and swiftly *Ps 89:3-4*
run after its spirit as [the spirit] does after
God. This is the rejoicing of a blessed people
knowing jubilation, walking in the light of
God's countenance,* exulting in his name, *Ps 89:15*
[a people] to whom the righteousness of being raised up is God and he himself is the
glory of their power.* For this is the taking *Ps 89:16-18*
up of the Lord and Our Holy King of Israel!* *Ps 89:18*
When we sense in goodness* him who has *Ws 1:1*
been made like to us, we sense in ourselves
what also is in Christ Jesus Our Lord,* for we *Ph 2:5*
are made like to him by suffering joyfully
with him now and afterwards we shall be like
to him by reigning with him.* *2 Tm 2:12*

There can be nothing in this life more
agreeable for man than for his well-*affected*
conscience[20] to find itself in the image of its
Maker and in the likeness of His goodness.
Anyone who desires this tenderness does not
by any means have an onerous, laborious compulsion in the exercise of faith, for tribula-
tion produces patience, and patience the
standing of the test, the standing of the test
indeed hope, but hope does not disconcert,* *Rm 5:3-5*
for after testing, charity is diffused in the
heart and soon this tenderness of a devout
mind is put in order by the Holy Spirit and he

becomes for it God's frequent visitation,
guarding, as the saintly Job says, the spirit of
Jb 10:12   your servant.* How could this visitation be
more tender, the consolation greater, the light
more divine for those hoping, for those sons
of light struggling in the darkness of this life,
Eph 1:18   than for the eyes of an enlightened heart*
somehow, sometimes, in a sudden flash of
illuminating grace, to see the one who shows
himself, to sense him who promises, to understand that the Lord is mercy and plentiful
Ps 130:7   redemption* and what that propitiation is,†
†*Ps 130:4*   to look up toward what has been promised in
the region of good for those [now] struggling
in the region of evil, to bring before the face
showing forth grace the face showing forth a
good conscience!

O, therefore, whoever you are, you who
desire and strive to have in your faith during
this life this joy, this brief abode of your Lord
God, do not be a doubter, do not be a waver-
er, but be an absolutely resolute governor of
your heart! Hold in resolute faith a resolute
joy on the foundation of a good conscience
and it will be yours and no one will take it
Jn 10:18   away from you.* Finally, after you begin to
see, take the trouble to see quite frequently.
May you sense more strongly that you may
begin to recognize it. From this there will then
begin to shine on the faithful person a new
sort of face of faith in the recognition of God,
one which promises itself in this life, yet gives
itself utterly in the life to come. It was about
this that the Lord, praying for his disciples,
said to the Father: This is eternal life, that
they may recognize you the true God and

him whom you have sent, Jesus Christ.*   *Jn 17:3*

31. There is one recognition of God that comes from faith, another from love or charity. That of faith belongs to this life, but that of charity to eternal life, or rather, as the Lord says: This is eternal life.* It is one thing   *Ibid.*
to recognize God as a man recognizes his friend, another to recognize Him as He recognizes himself.* General recognition is to have   *1 Co 13:12*
within oneself in one's memory the image* of   *image = phantasm.*
the person recognized or of a thing recognized, conceived from having somehow seen it; [by this image] the reality, when it is absent, can still be reflected on or, when it is present, be recognized. This recognition in respect to God is one of faith, not that it has some resemblance to an image but rather that it has the definite *affectus* of piety.[21] Derived from faith and confided to the memory [this *affectus*], as often as it turns again to the experience of the person who remembers, gently influences the conscience of the person who reflects. But the recognition which is mutual to the Father and Son is the very unity of both, which is the Holy Spirit. The recognition by which they recognize one another is nothing other than the substance by which they are what they are. Yet in this recognition no one learns to know the Father except the Son and no one learns to know the Son except the Father and him to whom He chooses to reveal Him.* These are the Lord's   *Mt 11:27*
words. The Father and the Son reveal this to certain persons then, to those to whom They will, to those to whom They make it known, that is, to whom They impart the Holy

CHAPTER SIXTEEN

The Presence of the Holy Spirit

Y ET THIS IS SO in one way in the divine substance wherein he himself* *the Spirit is consubstantially one with the Father and Son, but in another way in inferior matter. One way in the Creator, another way in creatures; one way in His own nature, another way in grace; one way in Him who gives, another way in him who receives; one way in the unchangeableness of eternity, another way into the changes of time. There, [in God] in the first way, the Holy Spirit, naturally and consubstantially, is mutual charity, unity, likeness, recognition, and whatever else is common to both. Here [in us], however, He accomplishes this in the person in whom He comes to be and by accomplishing this through grace is integrated in him. There the mutual recognition of the Father and Son is unity. Here it is a likeness of man to God; of it the Apostle John says in his epistle: We will be like to him because we will see him as he is.* *1 Jn 3:2

32. There, to be like to God will be either to see or to recognize him. One will see or recognize him, will see or recognize to the extent that he will be like Him. He will be like

Him to the extent that he will see and recognize Him. For to see or to recognize God there is to be like to God and to be like to God is to see or to recognize Him.

This perfect recognition will be eternal life: the joy which no one takes from the person who has it.* Here, [this joy] can never be full; it can only be made full in the full recognition of God, because those things about God of which one has knowledge or recognizes here can never be known or recognized as [they shall be] in that life when He will be seen face to face* as He is.†

*Jn 16:22

*1 Co 13:12
†1 Jn 3:2

This way of recognizing cannot be expected here from the mouth of any man, for it could not be learned from the mouth of truth himself.* It is not that the Lord could not have taught it, but that human weakness could not bear it. Yet even here he does not entirely withdraw it from those who love him and whom he has loved, to the end that they may know what they are missing.*

*Jn 16:12

*Ps 39:4 (LXX)

Over the impoverished and needy love of those poor in spirit and over what they love anxiously hovers the Holy Spirit, the Love of God. That is: he performs his works in them, not through the compulsion of any need but through the abundance of his grace and generosity. This was signified when he hovered over the waters,* whatever those waters may have been. As the sun hovers over the waters, warming and lighting them and drawing them to itself by its heat, by some natural force, that it may thereby furnish rains to a thirsty earth in the time and place of God's mercy, so the love of God hovers

*Gn 1:2

over the love of His faithful person by breathing upon and by doing him good, seizing to Himself the person who follows Him by some natural hunger and who has the natural ability of rising upwards like fire. He unites him to Himself so that the spirit of the person who believes, having trusted in God,* may be made one with Him.†

The Father and the Son are equally addressed by the same word:* for God is spirit.* It is also proper for the Holy Spirit to be particularly addressed by the same [word]: he who seems not so much [to be the spirit proper] to each of them as in fact their communality. The Holy Spirit himself communicates to man this word 'spirit', to the end that, according to the Apostle, the man of God may be made one spirit with God,* both by the grace of the name and by the effect of its power. It is not one person only but many persons who have one heart and one soul in Him, as a result of the sharing in this supreme charity at the source of which is the unity of the Trinity.

*Ps 78:8

†1 Co 6:17

*spirit

*Jn 3:24

*1 Co 6:17

CHAPTER SEVENTEEN

Union with God

AND SUCH is the astounding generosity of the Creator to the creature; the great grace, the unknowable goodness, the devout confidence of the creature for the Creator, the tender approach, the tenderness of a good conscience, that man somehow finds himself in their midst, in the embrace and kiss of the Father and Son, that is, in the Holy Spirit. And he is united to God by that charity whereby the Father and Son are one. He is made holy in Him who is the holiness of both. The sense of this good and the tenderness of this experience, as great as it can be in this miserable and deceptive life, although it is not now full, is yet a true and truly blessed life! In the future it will be the fully blessed and full life, unchangeably eternal; that means, when Paul recognizes as he is recognized,* when what is in part will have been done away with and what is perfect will have come,* when God will be seen as He is!† It is a dangerous presumption to look for the fulness of this knowledge in this life. In the same way, just as unbelief concerning what should be believed is to be avoided, so is rashness concerning what is to be understood. For

*1 Co 13:12

*1 Co 13:10
†1 Jn 3:2

the time being, authority governs faith, truth [governs] intelligence. For the time being, although God cannot be seen or recognized as He is, it advances the person advancing no little bit if he accepts nothing in God's place which is not God himself, so that this faithful mind shuts out and rejects anything physical or localized which occurs to it, or anything exhibiting a form of quality or dimension of quantity. Let the mind reflect on truth itself insofar as it can and let it recognize it with absolute certitude and love it. It discerns that this truth truly exists from the fact that it loves even a truth not reflected upon.

This truth is God, who is what he is, and from whom and through whom and in whom* is all that is. He is that supreme good from whom and in whom and through whom anything good is good. Take away from truth everything true, from goodness everything good and, if you can, reflect on that truth itself, that goodness itself. Who can ponder this and not love it? *Rm 11:36

Surely God is one and the same! To ponder him and to love him is the same! I say *him* and not *about him.* Many persons who do not love him, ponder *about him.* But no one ponders him and does not love him. We should always yearn to taste, insofar as it may be granted us, how sweet the Lord is.* When the devout mind, the humble mind, does not deserve to be admitted into that purity on account of its own impurity—or when, if it is admitted to taste it, it is not able because of its own feebleness to hunger to enjoy it—let it be driven out not without *Ps 34:8

sighs of love and tears of sorrow. Let it embrace the goodness and discipline of the Lord: goodness because what is unworthy is admitted there and discipline because what is cast out is thereby taught. And let it bear this patiently as long as it is being cleansed and let it make itself worthy to be admitted more frequently and to tarry longer—whenever and wherever it may deserve to dwell in eternity so that it can be in Christ,* where he is,† and to be in the Father with Him in whom He is.* This is not for this life but for the life in which He will be seen as He is: He will be seen, He will be recognized. He will not be believed in. Would that we understood what we are saying. They see this, they understand this—that blessed people who know rejoicing, who walk in the light of God's face.* We throw words around;* we are carried away with words and we are held back from what cannot be expressed by any words. And yet, nothing can be said about it except in words.

Words have their own form for signifying things in conversation, and they evoke images in the thought of the person speaking or hearing them. When they signify the forms and the things formed, they draw the mind outwards from its inner being to these realities of which they are the signs. When they are the signs of spiritual and divine realities, however, they send us inward, but within they only impede and cast darkness over the eyes of the mind. Once let in this way, words infect the mind with their imaginations so that things spiritual and divine for which there are absolutely no forms or images can scarcely be reflected upon

*Ph 1:23
†Jn 14:3

*Jn 10:38

*Ps 89:15
*Nos: PL=Non

without them.

For example:* What is 'God'? The name of fear. What is 'Lord'? It is the name of power. If you seek the name of reality itself, he says: I am what I am.* This name, as he himself says, is his from the beginning* because for signifying his reality, no word has ever come closer to him. But it does not express him as he is, for it passes by. What it signifies is eternal, and only the coeternal Word can fully signify that. It is all right, therefore, that many things have been spoken about him by many persons, but who can speak him save himself?

Yet love, enlightened love, which speaks inwardly to God, does this better [than words] as does humble devotion, whose striving is piety, whose approach is prayer, whose finding is understanding or the very enjoyment of the reality itself when our *affectus*[22] and grace converse, when faith and understanding correspond to one another, when hope and reality agree, when mercy and truth meet one another, when justice and faith kiss each other.* But because faith nourishes love, which heals the eye of the mind* to this end, let us grasp what we understand without obscurities. What we do not understand, let us believe without ambiguity. Let us not draw back entirely from using words, as long as by their assistance there is brought to us, who do not understand, that which we must perceive by words and yet believe without any form of words.

The Word of God has appeared for this reason in human form: so that as in many

*Literally: *In regard to words.*

*Ex 3:14
*Ex 3:15

*Ps 85:10
*i.e., reason. See ¶1.

and various ways God has spoken in times past to the fathers through the prophets, he might, in these most recent days, speak to us in his Son,* this is, effectually, as in his very Word itself, because what he has done in Him temporally and corporally he has extended to us to receive as with the hands of faith. He held out to those [who would] be purified through physical and temporal things that very Word through whom all things were made.* And for them, once they were purified, he has saved him to be possessed and contemplated in eternal blessedness. Just as there Christ will not be recognized according to a human point of view,* so here, too, those wanting somehow to recognize him beyond the man should not cling too hard to words about him but should rather pass over by them, as by a boat, from faith to vision.

*Heb 1:1-2

*Jn 1:3

*2 Co 5:16

If, when we say that the Father is in the Son and the Son in the Father* and that they are in us and we are in them,* we understand these words literally, what else are we making but an idol in our hearts? Although each has a place where he is, we stray far from the truth if, on the basis of these words, we think of a place or localization in God. Therefore, as I have said, either in words or in the forms of words one advances not a little if he accepts in God's place no reflections in his heart that are not God, in as much as God, as he is, cannot be conceived in thought. But although the Father is one person, the Son another, this is what it means that the Father is in the Son: that he is what the Son is. That the Son is in the Father means that he is what the

*Jn 10:38
*1 Jn 14:20

Father is. But we are in them through an ardent affection, while they are in us through the most merciful working of piety itself.

Both words of the Lord and this our explanation we have by use and reason taught our mouth to speak and our hearts to reflect as many times as we wanted to. Yet, however much we want to, we do not always understand them except through the experience of *affectus*[63] and an inner sense of an enlightened love.

Therefore just as the Lord himself, appearing in the flesh to men, took away from the world the vanity of idols, so too he proposed to those pondering God the unity of the Trinity and the Trinity in Unity. The glistening radiance of his divinity took away from any reflections of faith about God all vanity of the imagination. When he taught that the understanding of divinity is beyond men, he was teaching men to think in his own way. All the acts or words of the Word of God are for us therefore one word. Everything about him which we read, we hear, we see, we speak, we meditate on call us, either by provoking love or inculcating fear, to the One, sends us to the One of whom many things are said and nothing is said, because a person does not come to that which is unless He who is sought runs to him and shine His face upon us. May he shine his face upon us that in the light of his face* we may know how we are going.†

His face, revealing itself to the senses of the person who loves, is His will. His face is the recognition of his truth. Nor does anyone

*Ps 67:1,
Ps 89:15

†Plotius,
Enneades,
VI, 9, 4.

ever really sense God unless God is formed in him by this face or unless the sense of the person sensing God is conformed to His face. Nor does a person judge well by his senses unless the judgment of the person who judges grows out of that countenance.* Nor is anything done well, nor does anyone ever live well unless the actions and life of the person willing to live according to God are formed thereby. Neither is anything sought thereby except by the gift of grace which anticipates all deserving.

O You whom no one truly seeks and does not find, when that Truth for seeking you does not have in the conscience of the person who seeks a response that hints at some degree of the truth that is found, find us that we may find you! Come within us that we may go to you and live in you, for surely this comes not from the person willing, nor from the person running but from you who have mercy!* Inspire us first that we may believe! Strengthen us that we may hope! Call us forth and set us on fire that we may love. May everything of ours be yours 'that we may truly be in you,' in whom we live and move and have our being.**

§

*Ps 17:12

*Mt 7:7

*Rm 9:16

*Ac 17:28

1. Cf. Aenig 21 (CF 9:53) I am translating the Latin word *virtus* throughout as 'power' rather than as 'virtue'.

2. I have retained the Latin word *affectus* and have given a description and explanation of this word in the Appendix. *Affectus* is so technical in William's doctrine that it is difficult, if not impossible, for an English translation to capture the depth of its meaning and nuances. *Affectus* here means God's grace penetrating our soul and orienting her activities back to him by the particular and diverse operations of the individual powers (virtues) of faith, hope and charity.

3. *Affectus* in this case refers to the strong desiring element in our lives by which we become attached to God through sharing in his goodness.

4. Power, the translation for the Latin *virtus,* suggests the 'consubstantiality' of faith, hope, and charity. See ¶ 3 above.

5. *Affectus* of piety is the attachment of our soul, given to our Heavenly Father by the grace of a deep filial love, devotion and continual remembrance of him.

6. The *affectus* of faith is the power of faith as moved by our will permeated by the Holy Spirit, Charity, Love seeking understanding, in contrast to a faith based on only external authority.

7. The sensible knowledge coming from the body is transmitted to the soul; so William and Augustine teach. See CF 3, p. 106 footnote 31.

8. The Latin word is *palpitat.* In *Cant* (PL 180:520 C) a like phrase is found: *non ibi palpitabit fides.*

9. The Migne text reads: ' . . . *sed stupet ad insolita; non detrectans, aliquid scire appetens.*' The text of Déchanet and Davy reads: ' . . . *sed stupet ad insolita non detractans, sed retractans; aliquid credens, aliquid scire appetens.*'

10. Obscure sentence: The English omits the phrase *judicio quo noverat ipse.*

11. *Sense of Love* is explained by William in *Cant.,* Stanza 8, ¶ 94

(CF 6:76-7). In our vision of God 'love alone is operative without the cooperation of any other sense' and 'the vision of God is brought about in the sense of love by which God is seen'. This sense of love is the grace and understanding superaboundingly given to a soul who has turned to him in humble love. This grace and understanding culminates beyond the 'reach of any bodily sense, the consideration of reason, and all understanding except the understanding of enlightened love. In this state, for this man of God, there is no difference between grasping something of God and . . . becoming like him in accord with the nature both of the impression experienced and the love that experiences it'. See also paragraph 27 of the present text.

12.   The Latin word for religion is *religio,* derived from *religare:* to fasten or to bind. See Augustine, *The Greatness of Soul,* 36:80; *True Religion, LV,* 113; *City of God, X,* 3, 2; *Retractions, I,* xiii, 9.

13.   See William's companion treatise, *The Enigma of Faith,* CF 9.

14.   *Affectus* of imitating Our Lord Jesus simply means that the strong affective element in a person's life whereby he identifies and unites himself to another person is transformed by grace to such an intensity that in his imitation of Christ he will interiorize the very motivation (mind) of Christ even to the 'point of death on the cross'.

15.   This reference to *affectus* (for clarity, in the plural: *affectuses*) is important as it shows that we tend to God on various and different levels of our personality and soul structures. By the workings of grace— God's doing—these levels are gradually integrated and healed both to God and to one another by being integrated in God, resulting in a more mature and profound consciousness of God in our life.

16.   The *affectus* of love: our soul's love, penetrated by the presence of the Holy Spirit, so grasps our life, making us like a person in love continually having in mind the beloved, that nothing can separate us from our commitment and union to God.

17.   In order to bring out William's insight here, *clarificare* should be understood to mean both *to glorify* and *to make clear.*

18.   The *affectus* of devout faith is the power of faith as moved by our will, penetrated by the Holy Spirit [Charity] for the purpose of bringing forth in the dimensions of our humanity the 'making clear' of Christ's life. This 'making clear' has nothing of the Rationalists' philosophy of a clear and distinct idea. Rather, it is a sense of not obstructing Christ's shining forth in our relationship with him.

19a.   *Affectus* of devotion stresses our soul's unceasing and ardent activity to know and love God by an entire gift of self to him.

19b.   *Affectus* of love, under the impulse of the Holy Spirit, assimilates the individual into the One he loves, and thereby creates a mystical union (one spirit with God) which is, after a fashion, greater than the separate persons involved.

20.   A well-*affected* conscience, that is, grace elevating us into the

Word in the various levels of our whole person.

21.   See backnote 5. Recognition of God does not come from a mental image but from faith enlightened by that filial piety giving an understanding of God, Our Father.

22.   *Affectus,* here distinct from grace, is the soul in its concrete activity of desiring union with God.

23.   See backnote 19. The *affectus* is union with God (one spirit with God) which is more than a simple, ardent affection of God present in us by the working of piety.

APPENDIX

Affectus is so intricate a term in William's teaching that it is difficult, if not impossible, for a translation (English or other) to capture its meaning and nuances adequately. Translations of this word have ranged from near omission of it to an inconsistent rendering which results in a good disguise for the real depth and richness of William's thought.

William sees the deification of the human person as a penetration into our life of the Holy Spirit, the depth of God. By this penetration we love God and are loved by God; we become one spirit with God, love making us unable to will anything other than what God wills. This exchange of loving between God and ourselves, if it is to accomplish unity of spirit, must be an enlightened love. For enlightened love confers a way of thinking about God that is not at the disposal of the human person. Enlightened love confers a knowledge of God beyond human understanding and cognition. Enlightened love confers a recognition of God which is a sharing in the recognition that the Father has for the Son and the Son for the Father. *Amor ipse intellectus est.*

There is in our life a movement, a tending towards God. In its most human aspect this movement is our basic impulse to reach toward what is good; in its deified aspect it is either divine grace effective in the soul or the Holy Spirit himself praying within us a cry (*Abba Father*) that calls us into the depths of the Trinity. This movement towards goodness, found at the center of human attitudes yet incorporating 'something more than', 'something over and above' the human, is *affectus.* Between its human and deified aspects, the *affectus,* precisely because it is at the center of our life, can clothe itself in the various nuances of the powers (virtues) and faculties of our soul. In its tending to goodness, the *affectus* can be a movement of piety, or perception, or faith, or hope, or love, or thought, or will, and so on. Under an unusual influence and penetration of grace, the *affectus* can 'be' the Holy Spirit. William uses other words also related to *affectus,* such as *afficere, affici, affectio, affici deo, affici a deo,* etching either the divine or the human nuances of the mystery of the *affects.*

Speaking on the *affectus,* the German scholar W. Zwingmann says:

> The term is used nearly 250 times and covers several different meanings, but it may be said to indicate the deepest aspect of our tending towards God. On the one hand, *affectus* relates to the soul's ascent towards God (man is active); on the other, it also serves to designate the condescending grace of God, who stoops to the soul in search of Him (so that man, in a sense, is passive). It should be noted that in the second case the *affectus* is bound up with the work of the Holy Spirit. One may say that in the *affectus* God works in us and we co-operate in this divine action.[1]

While *The Enigma of Faith* is William's approach to understanding God's essence, *The Mirror of Faith* is his orientation to what contemporary language styles a mystical experience of God. A person who has glimpsed for a passing moment the vision of God that touches his affections,[2] begins to be as God is by entering into the foolish wisdom of the Passion of Jesus only to realize that he is becoming one spirit with God; he has an inability to will anything other than what God wills for his life. The route from faith to this unity of spirit is the *affectus:* the deepest aspect of a person's tending toward God, his goodness and blessedness. Responding actively and passively according to the workings of the Holy Spirit in the *affectus,* one is led to a recognition of God in faith. He is revealed first by authority and then by an understanding due to an inner illumination; one advances to the recognition of God, in an enlightened love that culminates in unity of spirit with him; that is, to the Holy Spirit forming of our spirit one spirit with God.

T. X. D.

---

1. For this translation of the passage I am indebted to Br Patrick Ryan's thesis, *The Experience of God in the De Contemplando Deo of William of St. Thierry,* (Ann Arbor, Michigan: University Microfilms International, 1977) p. 54.
2. William of St Thierry, *Ep Frat,* II, xviii, 268 ff.

ABBREVIATIONS

CF	The Cistercian Fathers Series
Comm	Commentary
Conf	The Confessions of Saint Augustine
Hom Ezech	Homilies on Ezechiel of Saint Gregory the Great
Moralia	Moralia on Job by Saint Gregory the Great
Pref	Preface
Solil.	The Soliloquies of Saint Augustine

WORKS OF WILLIAM OF SAINT THIERRY

Aenig	*Aenigma fidei. The Enigma of Faith,* translated by John D. Anderson (CF 9).
Cant	*Expositio super cantica canticorum. Exposition on the Song of Songs,* translated by Columba Hart OSB (CF 6).
Contemp	*De contemplando deo. On Contemplating God,* translated by Penelope Lawson CSMV (CF 3)
Ep frat	*Epistola ad fratres de Monte Dei. The Golden Epistle,*
Ex Rom	*Expositio in epistola Pauli ad Romanos. Exposition on the Epistle to the Romans,* translation by John-Baptist Hasbrouck OCSO (CF 27)—forthcoming.
Med orat	*Meditativae orations. Meditations,* translation by Penelope Lawson CSMV (CF 3).
Nat am	*De natura et dignitate amoris. The Nature and Dignity of Love,* translation by Thomas X. Davis OCSO—in preparation.
Nat corp et an	*De natura corpora et animae. The Nature of the Body and Soul,* translated by Benjamin Clark OCSO (CF 24).

Scriptural citations have been made according to the enumeration and nomenclature of The Jerusalem Bible.

INDEX

Numbers refer to pages in the translation